SWEET SATURDAY NIGHT

COLIN MACINNES

SWEET SATURDAY NIGHT

MACGIBBON & KEE

First published 1967 by MacGibbon & Kee Ltd
Copyright © Colin MacInnes 1967
Printed in Great Britain by
Cox & Wyman Ltd
London, Fakenham and Reading

For
BEATRIX MILLER

Contents

Contents

Deputy

WHEN the two red lights flashed on at either side of the proscenium arch to show the number of the next Music Hall turn, there was sometimes to be seen—ill-spelt in the globes or flares—the sinister word 'Deputy'. This meant that the advertised artist could not through some misfortune appear, and that to the immense dissatisfaction of the audience a substitute had been rapidly signed on by the management to fill as best he could the vacant position on the bill.

In some such guise I must appear to the reader, since I cannot speak with full and intimate knowledge of the great Music Hall stars. The classic era of the Halls was from about 1840 to 1920, so that anyone who was not an adult between those years—and such persons are now increasingly few—cannot describe something he personally knows well. Yet it has been possible for me to pick up many of the clues, and helped by these I shall try to evoke the rare and particular quality the old stars possessed.

I first became interested in Music Hall songs when I was three years old at a time when zeppelins were wobbling over London during World War I and when Florrie Forde (who hailed, surprisingly, from Australia) was singing—in a still recognizably Aussie accent—*Pack Up Your Troubles in Your Old Kit Bag (And Smile, Smile, Smile)*.[1] I had, in those distant days, a nanny; and on her afternoons off she and her friends would visit the Halls, and come back and sing the songs they'd heard to me in the nursery (or sing them during those visits to nanny's colleagues which, for bourgeois children at that time, were a sort of clandestine introduction to the

[1] Traditionally, the titles of Music Hall numbers are written with each word spelt in capitals. But as this is fatiguing to read, I shall put most of them in lower case from now on.

working-class world). Thus, long before I learned *God save the king,* or *Land of hope and glory,* or Protestant hymns, I recall that the first song I ever knew was *Tommy, make room for your uncle,* written and composed by T S Londsdale and sung by W B Fair—though this must already have been a revival of the number since Fair's dates are 1851–1909.

Nor was a knowledge of the Music Hall canon confined to the nursery. It is fairly well established that the middle classes didn't go much to the Halls—unless they were male bohemians like Sickert or intellectuals like Beerbohm—since the Music Hall art was almost exclusively working and lower-middle class both as to composers, singers and popular audiences. But many emancipated bourgeois households did know the numbers from sheet music, and these were sung round the piano in the family circle rather as the middle classes today might listen to a pop LP. In addition, with the curious and often noticed affinity of tastes between the extremes of populace and aristocracy, many of the most renowned of the Music Hall artists appeared privately in august drawing-rooms and indeed, since the Prince of Wales—the Edward VII one— was a considerable fan of the Music Hall art, at Sandringham as well, if not Marlborough House. Dan Leno, for example, became known as 'The King's Jester' on account of his popularity with the monarch, and there are many accounts of the tedium with which royal guests were compelled to listen to the jocosities of Harry Tate, while their delighted sovereign split his ample sides.

Thus, my maternal grandmother, who moved in what might be called intellectual upper-class circles, was a considerable addict. She was a particular fan of Little Tich's (more soon about him and other artists mentioned in this preface) and, as a girl, corresponded with this engaging and alarming dwarf. I don't think she ever went to the Halls herself though I know she did to pantomime where, as we shall see, many of the great Music Hall artists appeared at the Christmas season. I mention all this to suggest that although the atmosphere of my grandmother's house in London, where I spent my early childhood, was high-minded, not to say austere, I must have absorbed at a tender age much Music Hall lore: for with the strange duality by which stately Victorians enjoyed high-jinks, the Music Hall songs were not considered, as they might have been in more conventional houses, as reprehensible. (Though whether my grandparents, who were formidable survivals of the late Victorian era, recognized the frankly improper innuendo of so many Music Hall numbers, I wonder . . . though I'm inclined to think they did.)

My first direct encounter with the last of the great Music Hall artists took place when I was about seventeen, and had returned from Australia to England. We are now in the early 1930s, and by this time the Halls had already been dying for a decade, largely destroyed by the cinema, musical comedy and revue, and other technical and social causes which I shall suggest later more fully. But at the same time, a vogue for 'revivals' of the old artists had also begun, already strongly tinged with sentimental nostalgia. Thus, from their paupers' homes or affluent Brighton villas (for, as we shall see, Music Hall artists seem either to have been excessive spenders or savers), the old stars were hauled out of retirement to awake memories among old-timers, and to show their paces to a new generation addicted to ragtime, jazz (or what passed for jazz in England then) and the emerging talkies. By great good fortune a second cousin of mine, though still himself quite a young man, had been a Music Hall fanatic in his schoolboy and army days, and it was he who took me off to the Victoria Palace to hear such stars in their splendid decrepitude as Vesta Victoria, Harry Champion, Gus Elen, Fred Barnes and Alice Leamar.

Revivals of this nature continued sporadically into the 1940s and even the early 1950s—by which time almost all the classic stars had vanished. I hastened to any performance of this kind and, even at this late date, saw among others Kate Carney, Lily Morris, Talbot O'Farrell, Hetty King, Gertie Gitana, Billy Danvers, Nellie Wallace and Wee Georgie Wood. I mention these resounding names not so much to dazzle

11

the reader (though it must be admitted that to be able to say, as the late Esmé Percy used to when any contemporary actor was discussed, 'Ah, but he who has not seen Bernhardt . . .' affords a certain glow of spurious superiority) as to suggest that unless one has heard authentic Music Hall artists in the flesh it is almost impossible to conceive what they were like. I shall try to describe this later on; and meanwhile maintain that just as anyone who has heard only English interpretations of Negro blues singers, and not the original Negroes themselves, has no conception of how the real thing sounds, so no latter-day imitation of Music Hall artists comes anywhere remotely near the touching and impressive resonance of those lost voices.

By this time, I was getting rather hooked by the whole Music Hall thing—thereby arousing the mockery of friends to whom I revealed this passion, for they instantly imagined my growing interest in the Halls was that of a backward-looking nostalgiac. I am quite prepared to admit that my obsession was not exclusively that of the stern social historian, anxious to unfold the past to explain the present. Music Hall is indeed so anchored in a vanished epoch, and in its spirit so frequently sentimental (although, as we shall see, satirical and sardonic elements are equally apparent in it), that I do not think one could be deeply interested in the Halls without also feeling a regret that something so charming, innocent, comical and realistic has gone forever. Yet all this while my growing interest in the topic was matched by one in contemporary pop art, and at a time when few were yet writing about this (although everybody seems to be doing so now), I was also diving into teenage cellars and attending juvenile Sunday concerts in suburban super-cinemas in search of the modern equivalents of the Halls. And while I wrote often, in the 1950s, in such organs as would in those days deign to notice a phenomenon that has now become obvious to everyone, of the burgeoning of pop song among the young,[1] I have not, until this book, written much about the Halls. One discreditable reason, I suppose,

[1] See *England, Half English*, MacGibbon & Kee, 1962.

was that I feared that those who might accept me as a relent-
less investigator of the contemporary scene would lose any
faith if they found I was equally addicted to the arts of Gus
Elen, Dan Leno and Marie Lloyd. Yet what is manifest is
that the pop arts of both periods are equally revealing of
English *mores*, and that they are historically interconnected
in all sorts of ways shortly to be described.

Having heard something of the singers, I wanted to find
out if anything survived of the Halls. In the 1880s, there
were more than five hundred Music Halls in central London
alone—a figure not so surprising when one considers the
vaster number of cinemas that subsequently replaced them.
What had become of them, I wondered? What was the fate of
such gaudy popular palaces as the Britannia Hoxton, Bel-
mont's Sebright Bermondsey, The Falstaff Old Street, the
Grecian Saloon in the City Road Hoxton, the two Gattis
(Under-the-arches and Over-the-road by Westminster bridge),
the Cosmotheka, the Old Mo, the Paragon, the Pantheon and
the Surrey? So on my demobilization from the army in
1945, I decided, as an agreeable means of really getting to
know London, to track down the sites of these temples where
the art of the Halls had once flourished; and equipped with
a marked map and copious notes, I set forth in all directions.
As might have been expected, most had vanished; but some
survived as warehouses, cinemas, or in derelict solitude, and
a few actually lingered on as decrepit palaces of variety, like
the Queen's Poplar, Collins' Islington, The Bedford Camden
Town, the Metropolitan Edgware Road and the Granville
Walham Green. There were also still in existence a number
of variety theatres of later Edwardian vintage, like the
Hackney, Finsbury Park and Brixton Empires or the Chelsea
Palace, where something faintly resembling Music Hall tottered
on until television dealt these theatres their final death blow in
the 1950s.[1]

---

[1] Up till World War II, there were other variety theatres still open,
of which I shall speak when I come to describe, in the final section, the
swift decline of the Halls after World War I.

About this time, I started working free-lance for the BBC, and discovered that in its vast gramophone library which boasts that it can produce from its cellarage almost any disk (whether flat or even cylindrical) ever recorded (including a splendidly inaudible rendition by the laureate Tennyson of *Maud*), there was a large collection of old Music Hall records. Now unfortunately, the gramophone—and more particularly, electrical recording—came just too late to catch most of the great artists of the Victorian era although there do exist, for instance, recordings of Dan Leno who died as long ago as 1904. And what is more regrettable is that the gramophone, when it did appear, was regarded by most of the surviving Music Hall greats with deep suspicion, since they mistakenly supposed that, equipped with recordings, the public would no longer wish to hear them in the flesh; so that many of the best artists refused to have anything to do with this dangerous novelty at all. All the same, there do exist hundreds of records of many of the old stars, and I have spent long hours listening to their cracked, scratched and scarcely audible surfaces, trying to recapture their words and style—indeed, in one case I was able to rescue from oblivion, like a scholar poring over a tattered palimpsest, an almost incomprehensible song of great beauty of which no sheet music existed, by playing it over in sections dozens of times. Then, when electrical recording came, a few of the older artists who were still around were fortunately asked to the studios in their old age, so that there exist splendid and entirely audible recordings of such artists as Gus Elen, Harry Champion, Vesta Victoria and Tom Costello.

Anxious to discover more about the forgotten bards who wrote the words and music of these memorable songs (and as we shall see later, it turns out—as one might expect—that a relatively select few of them were responsible for the most famous numbers, even though these were sung by a variety of artists), and believing that the felicity of the tunes and lyrics greatly accounted for the popularity of the songs, I also spent much time in the equally massive BBC sheet-music library, in search of the composers and lyricists of the Waterloo

14

road which was, in the heyday of the Halls, the Denmark street of that time. And since the brilliant and charming coloured covers of the Music Hall song-sheets seemed the work of another group of pop artists whose talent matched those of the singers and composers, I spent much time in the Victoria & Albert museum's and other collections, trying to find out how contemporary artists envisaged the heroes and heroines whose delights, or more usually misfortunes, were celebrated in the songs.[1]

Thus equipped, I wrote in the 1950s a number of programmes for the BBC (sound) on Music Hall themes which involved tracing more songs and seeking out survivors of the Music Hall era. In a programme on Marie Lloyd there appeared Daisy Wood her sister, Marie Junior her daughter, Mrs Dick Burge her dresser, and among colleagues of Marie's her namesake Marie Kendall, Ella Retford, Ella Shields, G H Elliott and Albert Whelan. This was about the last authentic programme that could have been made at all—I mean one in which the veteran artists appeared in person— and not long after most of these old stars had gone. Later on, with Clarence Wright as singer and Alan Paul as pianist, we did six programmes under the general title of *The Boy in the Gallery*, in which we used what records could stand up to transmission, with Wright and Paul singing and playing songs which were too faded for the records to be audible, or had never been recorded by the original stars at all. The six titles of these programmes are those that I have used for the main sections of this study: a rather disordered, unscholarly way of assembling the material, but one which I think gives a clearer notion of the social relevance of the songs than would a chronological arrangement, and also perhaps matches the casual incoherence of the Music Hall art itself. These programmes were repeated many times—thereby confirming the

[1] May I pay grateful tribute to the microscopic memories of Miss Valentine Britten, of the BBC gramophone library, and of Mr Bill Sullivan of their sheet-music collection, who most kindly and patiently allowed me to borrow from their knowledge on countless occasions.

gloomy prediction of the BBC executive who (so a kindly spy told me), when the series was mooted, said, 'I'm afraid these programmes are going to be very popular.' For whereas a sociological approach to pop art is now commonplace, it was thought by 'educated' persons (such as then infested the BBC and no doubt still do) that any approach to past pop arts would be bound to be drenched in sentiment, and could not—which is what we aimed at—constitute an affectionate examination of what the old songs might reveal of English life during the eighty years the songs were sung.

Clarence Wright and Alan Paul, though both like myself too young to belong to the Music Hall era proper, had each an extraordinarily acute feeling for the mood of the old songs. This is extremely rare. I must once more warn the reader against brash and totally insensitive interpretations of these numbers that have been made by so many non-artists in latter years. From the late 1920s, when the 'Cave of Harmony' opened for the delectation of middle-class audiences, up till the ghastly club frolics of today which purport to recapture the authentic spirit of the Halls, performers of bourgeois origin have tried to sing these songs and failed abysmally. Their fatal error is both that they are patronizing in their attitude to the old artists, and that they inflict on the songs a vulgarity and over-emphasis they never had. The great Music Hall artists were robust yet extremely subtle. Their imitators lack vitality and tact—their heartiness is noisy and artificial, their 'wit' or sentiment leering and contrived. Their condescension is particularly revolting since not one of them could have stood up, in the flesh, beside the great artists they caricature without covering themselves with total ridicule and receiving, from popular audiences far more discerning than they can imagine, a well-merited bird.

But perhaps they are not altogether to be blamed. For no one, today, can sing the songs as the old artists did because the world from which these songs arose—which was proletarian, unselfconscious, poor, self-confident, crude, innocent and optimistic, however disillusioned—has forever vanished.

It was a world, however brutal, before great wars and revolutions, in which society of all classes was unaware of the latent forces that would soon erupt and destroy the old social fabric utterly. It was also a world before ragtime, jazz, the bioscope, radio, microphones, films and television—all of which have indeed produced astonishing artists in these media, but all of which, technically speaking, helped to destroy the older art of the Halls. To interpret these songs today, a certain degree of historical imagination and artistic discretion are indispensable. And the best that can be done to reproduce these numbers now is to approach them with extreme simplicity and respect, and take them as 'straight' as possible. This is what Clarence Wright and Alan Paul did so brilliantly: they tried neither to imitate, which would be impossible (anyone who has heard Harry Champion, for instance, will know why), nor to send up, which is all too dull and easy—they simply sang and played the songs in the mood which the vanished lyric writers and composers had intended.

Two other artists, neither of them English, helped in my education about the period: Yvette Guilbert and Grock. I saw both of them in their old age in the 'thirties, and in the art of Yvette one could catch the mood of the *café-concerts* of the 'nineties—the Parisian equivalent of the Halls—and in the art of Grock, see what a true clown could really be.

Yvette Guilbert had two styles—one the demurely impertinent manner of her improper numbers that have since been revived by countless French artists up till the present day; the other her 'naturalistic', slightly horrific style, in which she became a murderess, harlot, or a tragic victim of fatal illness or thwarted love. The wit, elegance, and precise throwaway timing of the first were beyond praise, while the second style, though it dated rather, could still be hair-raising in a melodramatic way. It is amazing to think that this self-educated artist, who once rivalled Bernhardt and the Duse in popular esteem, and who was admired the moment they saw her by such severe judges as Shaw and Sigmund Freud, should have developed her art among popular audiences in the pop theatre of her day. And I think we may discover that in Marie Lloyd the English Halls threw up a great artist of comparable stature who, while still in her 'teens, was at once recognized by 'illiterate' English audiences, without benefit of educated critics, as being a consummate interpreter of their daily lives.

The real clown is essentially subversive: he is not just a comic-pathetic like, for instance, Chaplin, but a person who thoroughly disturbs his audience by really making them wonder whether his world of upended logic is not in fact more real than their own sensible, ordered lives. Grock, of course, did 'funny' things to warm the audience up—the miniature fiddle, sliding down the piano lid and so forth—but he soon became an alarming, haunting figure. He always appeared with an immaculate stooge whom he insulted throughout his act. Driven to exasperation, the stooge would at last refuse to talk to Grock any longer. Grock continued to mock him, but the stooge remained obstinately silent. One then became aware that Grock himself was suddenly agonized by the thought that he was going to be isolated in his own mad world—abandoned by his sole human companion, and now utterly alone. So he began to appeal to the stooge, who still said nothing. The appeal at last became so painful that I have seen whole audiences riveted by this demonstration of our essential human isolation. Then Grock would make a crack, the stooge would be forced to laughter, and the tension would be broken. This was the voice of truth, as with Shakespeare's clowns, and in his performance, at moments, it quite got beyond being 'funny'.[1] Such an English artist, too, was Leno; and among dozens of Music Hall comedians, many of them brilliant, I believe he stands alone as a tragic clown who, like Marie Lloyd, lifted the whole boisterous, ramshackle art—and without ever losing for a

[1] What one might call Grock's 'theme word' was *Why?*—which meant more, because more drawn out, in *Pourquoi?* or *Warum?*: a word he used to question the whole reality of everything.

moment their roots in popular emotion—on to a higher and rarer plane.

If the student of Music Hall turns to the libraries, he confronts a desert: or rather, a cluster of tattered palm trees bereft of dates, with in the distance one refreshing oasis. The reminiscences are mostly of the 'those were the days' variety, packed with anecdotes about sharing a glass of bubbly with Harry Champion at the Derby, or eating whelks out of Vesta Tilley's shoe in a flower-laden brougham. The more 'serious' studies bury their subject under an accumulation of dated fact, are relentlessly uncritical, and seem to suppose that pop music ended when the Halls did. The biographies are mostly valueless—and here the biographers have certainly come up against an obstacle I have myself encountered when trying to entice recollections from old Music Hall artists, which is that they were both remarkably inaccurate (vowing, for instance, they didn't sing a song they most manifestly did), and deeply committed to their own legend and to those of their colleagues. Prudence thus dictates that all the delightful—and indeed highly plausible —tales one hears should be checked as far as possible with documented fact. As for the autobiographies, although I have gone so far as hopefully tracking Dan Leno into the British Museum, these are (except for rare shafts of rewarding light their authors have not succeeded—perhaps unconsciously—in hiding) usually public relations jobs, filled with bounce, japes and success stories. (Who would imagine, for example, if they knew only Dan Leno's own account of his career, that it was a profoundly sad one?) The great exception is M Willson Disher's *Winkles & Champagne*[1] which is an extremely sensitive and penetrating study, and the only really critical work on the Music Halls that has yet appeared. My own debt to it is endless.

A word of warning, before we take off, to those who do not care for sentiment. Almost without exception, English Music Hall songs are either sardonic or sentimental: life is a great

[1] Batsford, 1938.

big shame, as Gus Elen sang it, or a rose-tinted dream of
bliss. The taste of our day can accept the cynicism, but
entirely rejects the sentiment, so that many may find some
of the most cherished Music Hall numbers unbearably
saccharine.

Great art, of course, is never sentimental—but then, the
Music Hall art is not a great one: it was in many ways impure,
bridging a historic gap between a folk song that was quickly
dying, and a commercialized pop which has attained, in our
own day, to its mechanized apotheosis. All the same, I think
we can rightly distinguish between two sorts of sentiment:
the spurious moon in June synthetic variety, and then one
which does correspond to certain minor, yet authentic,
realities: old friends are better than new, there's no place
like home, if you were the only girl in the world and I was
the only boy, and so on . . . all these notions are banal, certainly, and yet real enough. And we might further remember
that a song whose lyric may seem soppy, and whose tune,
even if melodic, trite, and which will, if performed by a
singer who has no conviction about it, seem intolerable,
would, if sung as such songs were on the Halls, with total
and absolute faith, enshrine a serious spirit that redeems its
meagre theme. A verse of one of Marie Lloyd's earliest
numbers (it was really Nelly Power's in the 'seventies, but
Marie revived it a generation later and made it her own) runs,

Now if I was a Duchess, and had a lot of money,
I'd give it to the boy who's going to marry me;
But I haven't got no money, so we'll live on love and kisses,
And be just as happy as the birds on the tree.

Well, well! But if we could hear those commonplace words
with their soaring melody, sung by a vivacious, tender,
malicious girl with whom every young Cockney in her day
most certainly wanted to get into the tree (or elsewhere—and,
no doubt, accept the 'lot of money' to boot), we might feel
that the banality is somehow consecrated. Girls, after all, do

feel like that, even in the 1960s; though perhaps Marie would dream of being a Princess, not a Duchess, in our day.

Song is, I believe, a key indication of the nature and preoccupation of any people; and popular song, all the more so. Thus the Music Hall songs may complete whatever portrait we may have of an earlier era—as much, I think, by their reticences as by what they outwardly reveal. I think the reader will be mildly surprised to discover, if he doesn't know these songs, how much they disclose of Victorian and Edwardian life; and since they were chiefly written by, and sung by, working-class men and women for working-class audiences, we may hear in them a *vox populi* that is not to be found in Victorian and Edwardian literature.

Another strange quality they have is that though the men and women who first sang them are long dead, and although, as I have said, very few of them were recorded, and despite their not being sung all that frequently on radio or television and that not much sheet music exists, innumerable English men and women seem to know them. At a pub, or in a barrack-room, or at a convivial gathering of the kind where the hosts are called dad, mum, me sister or bruvver, one may hear them often: many of them have become the part of a folk memory, so that if you strike up *Lily of Laguna*, or *Daisy Bell*, or *My old man says 'Follow the van'*, everybody seems to know the words and music (that is, insofar as English men and women ever know the correct words and tune of anything).

How did younger generations learn them? It would seem as if, like nursery rhymes, and soldiers' songs, and certain hymns (and no doubt sea-shanties in their day), they are still handed down, from voice to ear, in families. I cannot otherwise account for the fact that *Lily of Laguna*, for instance, is perhaps still the best known song in England . . . despite the peculiar facts—typical of the oddity and absurdity of the whole Music Hall canon—that this apparently immortal English popular love lyric is about the passion of a Negro for a Negress, and was first launched in England by a blacked-up German–American called Eugene Stratton.

Love

LOVE is the favourite theme of the Music Hall songs, and it is either portrayed as a rose-capped dream of bliss, or as a comic disaster, different artists specializing in either version though some, like Marie Lloyd, could switch on occasion from the one mood to the other. Perhaps her prettiest song in the more hopeful vein is *The Boy in the Gallery* which, being a number dating originally from the mid-Victorian era, still preserves some of the deft simplicity of a folk song. It tells of a young girl who's just 'come over from the country', and she sings it to her Johnny, 'a tradesman who works in the Boro'' sitting up there in the gallery, listening. According to her sister, Daisy Wood, when Marie sang it, Daisy, stationed up in the gallery, would at the critical moment ('There he is—can't you see him? A-waving of his handkerchief') impersonate the young tradesman by doing precisely that.

Matilda Alice Victoria Wood was born in Peerless street, Hoxton, on 12th February 1870, the eldest of a family, three others of whom (Alice and Grace, called 'The Lloyd Sisters', and Daisy Wood) later became minor stars in their own right. Her father ('Brush' Wood) was a waiter at the Grecian Saloon, a pub and theatre in the City road which grew in 1881 to be the Royal Eagle Music Hall. (Hence the ditty, 'Up and down the City Road, in and out of the Eagle'. A pub of the same name—but rebuilt in Edwardian days—stands on the site of the old Hall). The proprietor of the Royal Eagle was, most surprisingly, General Booth of the Salvation Army; for the General had bought for the Army a property of which the Eagle tavern was a part, and by the terms of the lease he could not close it. Marie was already a singer of a sort when at the age of seven she joined the Band of Hope, and under her father's careful eye she was able to watch the performers at the Eagle while he served the clients.

Her début, at the age of fifteen in 1885, was at the Falstaff Old street, where she appeared (so Daisy Wood tells us) in one of her mother's dresses and under the improbable name of Bella Delmere, singing *The Boy in the Gallery* (words and music by George Ware) which became an overnight success. By the time she was sixteen she was married and a star, and may I here digress (as I fear I shall constantly) to point out that the notion that teenage stars are a contemporary novelty is quite mistaken, since almost all of the great Music Hall artists were well away before they were twenty. An astute manager advised her that 'Bella Delmere' was an even more unsuitable name than Matilda Wood, and Marie chose 'Lloyd' because *Lloyd's Weekly* was the *News of the World* of its day, and she thought everyone would remember the name. She picked Marie (pronounced Máh-ree) as a first name because she liked it.

In the 'eighties she played most of the big London Halls, and if this seems remarkable, it was possible because an artist much in demand used to appear at several Halls on the same evening. Music Hall was, essentially, a performance made up of single acts with no kind of continuity as in musical comedy or revue. Having finished at one place, the artist would leap into a brougham and dash off to the next theatre, even playing as many as four Halls in one night. This must have been harassing for the theatre managers (as well as exhausting for the singers), but it also meant that a new artist would be rapidly projected throughout the capital.

The 'nineties were her great decade when she played for a year non-stop at the Oxford (now a Lyons Corner House) and starred in Christmas panto at Drury Lane. She was never loved outside London (nor much liked leaving it), and it was in Sheffield ('the comedians' graveyard') that, for the first time in her life, she got the bird. She waited till the row sub-sided, refusing to leave the stage, and then thus addressed the audience: 'So this is Sheffield: this is where you make your knives and forks. Well, you know what you can do with them, don't you. And your circular saws as well.' It was perhaps sallies of this kind, and her general reputation for indecency, that led to one of her rare disappointments in London, that of not being invited to the first Royal Variety performance at the Palace theatre in 1912.

She was three times married, first to Percy Courtney (the father of Marie Junior) whom she divorced in 1904; then to Alec Hurley, a fellow artist ('The Cockney King') whom she adored till his death in 1913; and at last—and fatally—to Bernard Dillon, the jockey, when she was forty-three and he in his early twenties. This was a thoroughly unhappy marriage, and with failing health, the disruption of World War I, and swift changes in Music Hall fashions ('ragtime' was by now all the rage) she was a fading star when her fiftieth birthday was celebrated at the Bedford Camden Town, in 1920. She collapsed during a performance two years later, and died leaving only insurances after earning a fortune exceeding a hundred thousand pounds. At her death, the taps on the bars round Leicester Square were draped in black, and 100,000 Londoners watched the coffin leave her house in Golders Green. First came the hearse, which passed in respectful silence. Then came a carriage with the young widower, sitting alone, amid groans of disapproval from the populace. When the family coaches next passed by, there was solemn silence once again.

Throughout her career, she had two chief styles—which can be seen portrayed on either side of the sign outside the pub named after her in Hoxton. In the first, she was the pretty, vivacious, naughty Cockney girl, mildly indecent, though never crude or vulgar. She wore, according to Marie Kendall, 'a white lace dress, with pink and blue ribbons and her golden hair right down there, natural . . . and her big blue eyes and her tiny baby's cap of lace. And she came on with a hoop, and looked like a toy doll'. As she grew older she became rather 'grand' in this style and, so Ella Retford tells us, wore 'a fabulous gown that was slashed up to the waist and showed pink silk tights . . . with a wonderful diamond garter. And she had the smallest little hat over one eye—the one she used to wink—and the largest paradise I have ever seen—pink. And don't forget the stick. A long, long cane all studded with diamonds'. Marie was five feet two inches ('semi-petite, with beautiful limbs' says Marie Kendall), her teeth were 'beautiful and rather prominent' and Ella Retford speaks of 'the way she handled her beads . . . and rubbed them across her teeth with that saucy look and that wonderful smile'.

Max Beerbohm tells us that 'she had an exquisitely sensitive ear for phrasing and timing', though her fellow artists admit that her voice itself was not remarkable—'a bit on the gruffy side' according to her daughter, Marie Junior, and her sister Daisy Wood tells us that 'Marie never had what you could call a good voice. When she sang a song, she was in it. She got into the words. She was the character. And every word you could hear'. The 'gruffy' yet precise and audible voice sustained her in her second style, that of the later 'character' songs in which she portrayed Cockney disasters, usually of a lugubrious nature. In *I'm one of the ruins that Cromwell knocked about a bit* she compared herself to the Abbey after the Lord Protector had finished with it, and it was while staggering about the stage in this number, apparently in the last throes of comical decay and dementia, that she in fact collapsed a few days before her death. In *My old man says, 'Follow the van'* (by Charles Collins and Fred W Leigh), also known as *The Cock-linnet song*, Marie portrayed a forlorn spouse abandoned by her husband who's gone on ahead with the moving van in which there's no room for her. Marie follows dolefully behind, carrying her pet bird in a cage, and disobeying her old man's injunction not to 'dilly-dally on the way', she stops at so many pubs that she forgets the new address and 'can't find my way home'. Among her earlier, but perhaps less remembered, 'pretty' songs are *Oh, Mr Porter, When I take my morning promenade* (much use of the diamond-headed cane in this one) and *A little of what you fancy does you good* by Fred W Leigh and George Arthurs. As she grew older, her songs were *Put on your slippers* (*you're here for the night*) and *I'm a thing of the past, old dear.*

Oh, Mr Porter (music by George Le Brunn, lyric by his brother Thomas) may explain to us why it was that Marie was constantly in trouble—to the delight of her public—with the authorities. The chorus of this ditty could not seem more innocuous:

Oh, Mr Porter, what shall I do?
I wanted to go to Birmingham and they've carried me on to
    Crewe . . .
Take me back to London as quickly as you can,
Oh, Mr Porter, what a silly girl I am!

But as Marie played it, something sensationally disastrous happened between Birmingham and Crewe, and the reason why she's a 'silly girl' who must get rapidly back to London is all too painfully apparent. But though she was summoned before a committee of the LCC to answer the unfavourable reports they'd heard of her, she thwarted them by singing her own songs absolutely straight to them, and then by maintaining that the sort of poetry *they* liked was in fact more reprehensible. To illustrate this, she chose *Come into the garden, Maud* singing it loaded with innuendo, and demanding what did he want her in the garden for, and what was he doing when he said, 'I'm here at the gate alone.' All the same, though Marie was improper she was never lewd, and one is irritated to hear smutty numbers attributed to her she never sang at all, or 'Marie Lloyd stories' which, if one meets her family, are inconceivable (chiefly because they're so feeble). With Marie, it was all a question of taste and tact. Or, as she sang herself, 'Ev'ry little movement has a meaning of its own, Ev'ry little story tells a tale'—and whatever else they were, these had to be attractive and amusing.

    Every account confirms that she was an immensely attractive personality—indeed, those I have heard who knew her become rather incoherent trying to make this plain. Her reckless generosity, her spontaneity, her laconic wit, her thoughtful affection, and her restless animal spirits were all emphasized. Also her simplicity. Marie Kendall tells us that her favourite repast, when she was earning hundreds of pounds a week, was 'smoked haddock with an egg' and 'light ale out of a little silver tankard'. Mrs Dick Burge, her dresser, recalls that 'her favourite bit at night was a piece of bread and dripping, with red gravy from the bottom of the basin'. Yet she loved finery, and Marie Kendall remembers her at Ascot wearing 'a remarkable dress of *broderie anglaise* with a touch of blue and a great hat with plumes'. There seems also to have been a streak of melancholy, a reluctance, often, to face audiences that idolized her; and though she never disguised her age, a horror of growing old. 'Happiness,' said Ella Retford, 'was the one thing that seemed to pass her by.'

Of her songs, it is quite impossible to judge by the few surviving recordings: these are all pre-electric, and pretty dreadful. It is clear, also, that she depended enormously on the personal 'projection' of her numbers, so that even a faithful recording would probably miss what was most important. Yet we are forced to believe not only infatuated old-timers, but artists like Sarah Bernhardt who declared she was 'the only woman of genius on the English stage' (though perhaps this was just to be bitchy to the others) and Beerbohm, who bracketed her with the Queen and Florence Nightingale as the three most memorable women of the Victorian age.

My own guess is that she personified, for Londoners in her day, the good-bad girl that most women would like to be, and every man would like to have: the girl who is flighty, alluring, and physically attractive, yet wise, understanding and basically reliable. She may also have embodied, for Cockney working-class audiences, a woman of such style, glamour and general splendour as to make them feel no duchess was finer than 'Our Marie', as they grew to call her. Insofar as she remains a legend to Londoners, I think it is in somewhat the same way as Nell Gwynne does: their own girl who made the grade, wasn't over-impressed by her 'betters', had her own true elegance and wit and, so far as conduct goes, put the best things first in her priorities of good and evil.

Kate Carney, a contemporary of Marie Lloyd's— she was born in 1869, and lived on until 1950—was also a singer of the more fulsome kind of love ballads, yet her delivery made these seem exceedingly astringent because she bawled out her ecstasies like an amorous foghorn. One of the rare Jewish singers among the Music Hall greats, she was the bard of Stepney, and *Has anyone seen my Yiddisher boy?* was one of the most popular numbers in the Whitechapel Halls.[1] But her two most remarkable songs are *Are we to part like this?* and *Three pots a shilling.* In the first, she reproaches Bill, her lover, with abandoning her for 'another' and challengingly demands (in tones to shake the crystals from the gallery chandeliers), 'Who's it ter be—'er or me, Don't be afraid to say!' Like so many Music Hall love songs it is in waltz time, and if one heard only the tune—which is an exceedingly

[1] Though there may have been few Jewish singers, as there were also fewer impresarios in the Music Halls than in the theatre as a whole, there was certainly an indirect Jewish influence on the Halls, of two kinds. As regards audience, the Jewish public has always supported the popular theatre disproportionately to its numbers—it still does. As to the whole East End Cockney ethos, this is impregnated with Jewish speech, feelings, even looks. The Jewish community of recent immigration (that is, apart from the Sephardic Jews who arrived in England much earlier) dates, so far as the East End is concerned, from about 1880 when the first big migrations to England started, to 1945, by which time most East London Jews—as indeed a large part of the Gentile population—had, because of World War II and growing prosperity—abandoned the classic East End.

Yet when one reflects that large Jewish communities lived around Stepney for about sixty years, it is not surprising that the Jewish influence on Gentile life was great. And though most Jewish boys, since families were still orthodox, married Jewish girls, there was no ban on love affairs with Gentile girls (single or married) and there must have been thousands of these unions, and many children born of them. One may thus see, round about Stepney, boys and girls of technically Gentile families who have an unmistakeable Jewish style about them, and this is one of the many attractions of the East End lad or bird. Jewish vivacity, sentiment and sexual skill add a kind of salt and pepper to the native East End dish. Further north, or south of the river, the Cockney character, though robust and vivid, hasn't got the same style and spice.

pretty one—or read the lyric without hearing Kate, one might suppose it to be a decorous ditty. But not as she yelled it! Though curiously, even though you felt Kate Carney could knock Bill down if he denied her (she was a short stocky woman and looked capable of it), she does infuse a genuine lyricism into her harsh delivery. Incidentally, it seems an article of faith among revivalists of Music Hall songs that the singers added an accented 'ah' to the end of any line. Of all those I have heard in person or on record, only Kate Carney did this, so the imitators must have picked up the trick from her, Thus, with her it became

Who's it ter be—ah . . . 'er or me—ah?

a device which she uses to reinforce her threat to Bill.

Three pots a shilling (also a waltz number, and a delightful one, with music and lyrics by Harry Bedford) is one of the many coster songs that were beloved of Londoners. The costers—who now survive in a ghostly sort of way in the form of Pearly Kings and Queens—were important London figures in Victorian England, living mostly south of the river in the heyday of the Halls (though they emigrated originally from the east), and who drove in their donkey-shays with fruit, vegetables and flowers to sell at Covent Garden and suburban markets. Throughout the year the London streets were suddenly filled by their mass migrations: on Easter Monday to Hampstead, on Derby Day to Epsom, on August Bank holiday to the Welsh Harp—a lake formerly of that shape—at Hendon, and throughout the summer Saturday nights they descended in droves on Peckham Rye. They are always portrayed as vehement, independent characters and indeed, being small capitalists rather than wage earners as most Londoners were, they formed a sort of proletarian élite.

In Kate's song about the Three Pots, the coster boy is telling his girl how when the summer comes, they'll make their fortunes and get wed. Through it there run two minor themes that recur perpetually in Music Hall numbers, the

29

one a nostalgia for the country (which in fact, as we shall see later, they were extremely reluctant to visit, and from whence they fled whenever they happened accidentally to get there), and the other, the realistic insistence on the absolute importance of money. The lack of this among the working classes in Victorian and Edwardian England is of course obvious enough, but it is striking how even in love lyrics its importance is frequently underlined. The verse in fact, opens on this note:

> Oh, won't we have some money, dear,
> When the summer comes again . . .

And at the end of the resounding chorus, the coster is reminding his girl of the need for a customer for his 'pots' (of flowers):

> I shall cry, she shall buy
> Three pots a shilling!

The artist known as 'The Costers' Laureate' (though not, one imagines, by the costers themselves) was Albert Chevalier (1861–1923) who is something of a curiosity among Music Hall artists, since he was a gent (or semi-gent) born not, like most of the London singers, in the east or south, but in Notting Hill. We shall meet soon with genuine coster singers—like Gus Elen—who sang whereof they intimately knew, but Albert Chevalier (no relation, by the way, to Maurice, though Maurice Chevalier told me he knew his namesake's act) was really a sort of artist-sociologist who scanned the Cockney scene as an outsider, and wrote and sang songs about it. The invasion of the variety world by gentlefolk is now quite a familiar phenomenon, but in Chevalier's day it was exceptional. He was thus one of the few artists well known to the middle classes, for towards the end of his career he abandoned the Halls and gave 'recitals' from the concert platform. He was quite a success, too, in America, where his diluted rendition of 'Cockney' humours was found acceptable, and no doubt helped to contribute to that mis-reading of the Cockney character which still seems general in the States (or in England too, for that matter).

It is hard to write of Chevalier without great admiration and intense nausea. He was an astonishing lyric writer and composer, and songs like *The future Mrs' Awkins, Knocked 'em in the Old Kent Road* and the appalling but irrepressible *My old Dutch* are undoubtedly Music Hall immortals. But his style, as described disdainfully both by Shaw and Beerbohm, and as it still comes over horribly on recordings, is revolting: drenched in cloying sentiment, the words dragged out with sickening over-emphasis. But he has some wonderful lines. From *The future Mrs' Awkins*:

If yer die an old maid you'll 'ave only yerself to blame . . .

And *The Coster's Serenade* (written in collaboration with J Crook), in which the lovelorn boy, in winter, remembers the happy summer days with his girl at the Welsh Harp, is a little masterpiece: the words apt and easy, and the tune—which rises, at the end, to a harassing crescendo—perfectly fitted to the mood and theme:

You ain't forgotten yet that night in May,
Down at the Welsh 'Arp which is 'Endon way:
You fancied winkles, and a pot of tea,
'Four 'alf,' I murmured's, 'good enough for me.
Give me a word of 'ope that I may win,'
You prods me gently with the winkle pin—
We was as 'appy as could be that day,
Down at the Welsh 'Arp, which is 'Endon way.

Oh! 'Arriet, I'm waiting, waiting for you my dear . . .
Oh! 'Arriet, I'm waiting, waiting alone out 'ere . . .
When that moon shall cease to shine,
False will be this 'eart of mine;
I'm bound to go on lovin' yer, my dear,
D'you 'ear?

31

Nor can it be denied that *Knocked 'em in the Old Kent Road* is a
telling social vignette with, once again, a tune of Chevalier's
that is still rightly remembered. The theme here is another
recurrent one—that of the unexpected inheritance, a veritable
obsession with Music Hall lyric writers as it was no doubt with
their audiences too.

The great master, however, of the sentimental love ballads
was a composer, not a singer—Leslie Stuart. His real name
was Thomas Barrett, and he has some claim to be a 'serious'
light composer since his musical comedies, like *Florodora*
(much admired by Scott Fitzgerald—or at any rate by his
characters), have more than period charm, and the best songs
he wrote for the Halls are still delightful. His chief interpreter
was Eugene (Gene) Stratton (1861–1918) whose real name
was Ruhemann, and whose parents had emigrated to the
United States from Alsace. Stratton had come to England
with Haverley's Minstrels, and stayed on with the Moore and
Burgess troupe before drifting into the Halls.

I shall speak of the American Minstrel troupes in a moment,
and of their great influence on the Music Hall art, but first
to explain why Stratton became known as 'The Idol of the
Halls' and one of the most admired male artists. The first
reason is that Stuart gave him such memorable songs: *Lily
of Laguna* is of course the most famous, and *Little Dolly Daydream* runs it close. It couldn't have been the voice, for
Stratton hardly had any, and 'says' his songs more than
sings them. But the great appeal of his numbers was the soft-
shoe dance that accompanied them. If you hear the full score
of *Lily of Laguna*, for instance, you will notice that Stuart
has written in a long—and highly effective—passage without
words, during which Stratton drifted about the stage like
thistledown. Soft-shoe dancing has so entirely disappeared
that it is hard to visualize the effect Stratton's performance
had on enraptured audiences, but elderly connoisseurs of
his art speak of it in terms as ecstatic as those of ancient
balletomanes reminiscing about Nijinsky. In all his numbers
he appeared as a (judging from the photographs) highly un-

convincing Negro, and the songs themselves have all exotic settings—Little Dolly Daydream, for example, is the 'Pride of Idaho', and as for the immortal Lily, Leslie Stuart assured enquirers that Laguna did indeed exist—'If you are going from New Orleans to California,' he explained, 'it lies about a hundred miles to your left.'

It is difficult now to envisage whites impersonating what purported to be Negroes without a certain revulsion. (Or perhaps it isn't, since in England today the 'Black and White Minstrel Show' is exceedingly popular.) Nevertheless, we must try to situate an artist like Stratton in his period. The word 'Nigger', now absolutely tabu among enlightened whites (though used among themselves by Negroes), did not have, in late Victorian England, the pejorative implications it did in the States, and has since come to have over here. It was of course patronizing, but not more so than 'Paddy' or 'Taffy'. And it is certain that when audiences went to see a blacked-up artist, what they went to see was someone who appeared to them either glamorous—as in the case of Stratton—or 'improving', as in the case of the more soulful 'Nigger Minstrel' ballads. That there was also a marked comic element in the Minstrel performances is undeniable, but in laughing at supposed Negro rusticities there was no more mockery than there was in the laughter at comics of our own—for instance, George Formby Senior, who habitually portrayed English innocents.

The Nigger Minstrel period (I shall drop the inverted commas, for that was what they *were* called) almost overlaps that of the Music Halls, though it both began and ended rather earlier: 1840 to 1900 would be about the dates. The Minstrel troupes played in concert halls, like the St. James's in Piccadilly or the Agricultural at Islington, and were considered a much more decorous entertainment than the Halls, catering for family parties rather than the more vulgar populace. But though the two kinds of audience remained separate, there was a good deal of cross-fertilization among the artists, particularly among the Negro impersonators like

Stratton and the equally celebrated G H Chirgwin ('The White-eyed Kaffir'—of whom more later) both of whom came from the Minstrels to the Halls. Indeed, among the many sources from which the Music Halls sprang at the middle of the century, the Minstrel shows were one of the most important: if for nothing else, because they popularized the notion of public entertainment to those classes for whom the theatres, in general, did not cater.

Among the earliest troupes to arrive here from America were *McNish, Johnson and Shawn's*, who specialized in morbid and lugubrious numbers. The *Mohawks*, who offered Operatic Nights, Classical Nights, Military and Nautical Nights, and Sacred Concerts. The most illustrious American minstrel of all, Edwin P Christy (d 1862) never visited England, but former members of his troupe came to the St James's as early as 1859. Here they were joined by others, including George Washington (Pony) Moore who, in partnership with Frederick Burgess, founded the *Moore and Burgess Minstrels*. Thereafter there were numerous commutations, and by 1900 the most solid surviving troupe were the amalgamated *Mohawk, Moore and Burgess Minstrels*. The Minstrels spread from London to the provinces, and seaside resorts, particularly St Leonards, were favourite stamping-grounds.

Typical ditties—interspersed with witticisms by the Interlocutor—will give an idea of what their audiences admired. As well as sturdy American standards like *Nelly Bly, Old Folks at Home, Camptown Races* and *Jeanie with the light brown hair*, they were also treated to *Creep into bed, my baby (or one little kiss for Mamma), Heap pretty flowers on my grave, Kiss me, Mother, ere I die* and *Tears are blessings, let them flow.* A great many songs originating in the Minstrel shows — as *Willie, we have missed you, Close the shutter, Willie's dead* (Willie seems to have taken a beating at the Agricultural Hall)—found their way into the vast repertory of ballads sung round the piano in suburban homes, which many mistake for Music Hall numbers. But the key test of an authentic Music Hall song is that it was first sung by a named artist at a known Hall. And though some were sung in both places when artists like Stratton abandoned the sedate Minstrels for the rowdy Halls, the two types of song, although contemporary, are really quite different, since the Music Hall numbers have infinitely greater realism and vivacity. (Thus if one knows both arts, and hears a new number for the first time, it is almost always possible to tell from which it originated simply because of its melodic and verbal tone.)

It will now be seen that the influence of American popular singing on our own is by no means a recent phenomenon: it is, in fact more than a hundred years old. Sometimes the emphasis has flowed one way—from America when the Minstrels arrived, for instance, or in the American musicals of the 1940s and 1950s—sometimes the other, as when the English Music Hall artists invaded the States round the turn of the century and sang to packed houses and before Presidents, or in the vogue for English youngsters of today. Some artists have left one country for the other, like Stratton himself and Ella Shields, a Philadelphian renowned for her 'Cockney' numbers, or vice versa like Chaplin and Stan Laurel who began in the English Halls and made their big reputations in the States.

The last survivor of the influence of the Nigger Minstrels in our country was the late G H Elliot ('The Chocolate-coloured Coon') who could still be seen sometimes as recently as a few years ago. Although his own favourite was *I used to sigh for the sil'vry moon* he also sang Leslie Stuart numbers originally written for Stratton, though always punctiliously telling his audience that Eugene was their true begetter. To see, as late as the 1950s, a blacked-up white pretending to be a coloured man, and singing a love song to his Lindy Lou (who was in fact G H Elliott's plump and charming wife), was an amazingly archaic spectacle, though the Chocolate-coloured Coon carried it off with the utmost dignity and aplomb. As for Leslie Stuart himself, fate was less kind, for after World War I his songs were momentarily forgotten, and thousands who knew his *Lily of Laguna* did not realize that its creator was still among them. In the 1930s, he appeared at the Palladium and, alone at the piano and without explanation, played over numbers everyone in the audience remembered. As it dawned on them that Stuart had written them all, he was interrupted by an ovation.

It is with a measure of relief that one may turn to the more congenial description of the sardonic vision of love among Music Hall artists: certainly one most of its artists preferred, and whose dirges they sang enthusiastically in countless telling numbers. For as Orwell has pointed out, love, for the English working classes, is not to be reconciled with the aftermath of wedding bells: up till that fatal point, all is bliss; once the boy and girl become Dad and Mum, there is only resignation or disaster.

The situation may be symbolized by the title of one of Gus Elen's best numbers, *It's a Great Big Shame*. Ernest Augustus Elen was born in 1862 and died in 1940—his great age and energy enabling him, most fortunately, to record electrically, so that many of his best numbers are preserved for us. He is everything Albert Chevalier wanted to be, and was not: a dyed-in-the-wool Cockney with a voice of extreme authority, disillusionment and sardonic irony. Cockney speech, of course, changes from one decade to another, and what passes for 'Cockney' on the stage or television is often either dated or, if in period, inaccurate. But since Elen presumably spoke as an adult as he had learned to speak as a boy, it is possible to hear, in his strident, emphatic, sarcastically humorous voice, what a Cockney of a hundred years ago really sounded like.

The music of *It's a Great Big Shame* was written by George Le Brunn,[1] and the lyric by Edgar Bateman: one of the most fruitful of the Music Hall teams who wrote some of the best songs for a variety of artists in quite different styles. These

---

[1] Both Elen's and Le Brunn's names are often mis-pronounced. It is 'Eelen', not 'Ellen', and 'Le Broon', not 'Le Brun'.

songs came into being in four separate ways. Sometimes the actual singer was also his own bard: as Chevalier was or, most notably, Harry Lauder. Sometimes one non-performing artist wrote both words and music, as did Leslie Stuart. Sometimes there were teams of lyric writer and composer, as in the case of Bateman and Le Brunn. In yet other cases, both words and music would be written, in collaboration, by two or even three hybrid bards, each acting as both lyric writer and composer—as is the case with Harry Castling and Charles Collins, who jointly wrote *Are we to part like this?* for Kate Carney. I shall have more to say about these astonishing artists later on—hoping to rescue them for a moment from oblivion, for whereas the names of many of the singers are remembered, the poets and musicians who supplied endless and often highly effective material for them are now often completely forgotten. Yet when one considers that these teams of lyric writers and composers produced songs in their thousands for hundreds of singers, and that some consistently wrote the best songs for the greatest artists, theirs is an essential contribution to the Music Hall canon. A vast quantity of this output scarcely survived its period, and did not deserve to; just as there were innumerable singers whose faces we may find on dusty song sheets, but whose names are not even known now to connoisseurs. For the demand for new songs was, in those days (when there was no alternative whatever to the pub except the Halls for popular entertainment), insatiable; and those singers, lyric writers and composers who have still, more or less, survived in the public memory, were but a fragment of the whole vast production—which was almost, in the heyday of the Halls, an industry.

It's a Great Big Shame can, I think, best speak for itself Here are the first verse and chorus:

I've lost a pal, 'e's the best in all the tahn,
But don't you fink 'im dead, becos 'e aint—
But since 'e's wed 'e 'as 'ad ter knuckle dahn—
It's enuf to wex the temper of a saint!

'E's a brewer's drayman wiv a leg o' mutton fist,
An' as strong as a bullick or an 'orse—
Yet in 'er 'ands 'e's like a little kid—
Oh! I wish as I could get 'im a divorce.

It's a great big shame, an' if she belonged ter me
I'd let 'er know who's who—
Naggin' at a feller wot is six foot free,
And 'er only four foot two!
Oh! they 'adn't been married not a month nor more,
When underneath her fumb goes Jim—
Oh, isn't it a pity as the likes of 'er
Should put upon the likes of 'im?

Philologists who doubt whether Cockneys really did ever
substitute w's for v's will find that Gus Elen confirms that,
like Sam Weller, in the 1860s, they did. The Cockney use of f
for th, of course, still exists (and sometimes of v for th,
though this is not illustrated in the song—as with 'bruvver'
for 'brother'). Another peculiarity is that Elen pronounces
'put' in the last line as if the word were 'putt', in golf.

Billy Merson (in fact William Henry Thompson), born 1881,
died 1947, is remembered only by one song—of which he
wrote the words and music himself: *The Spaniard that blighted
my life*. All foreigners in the Music Hall world are, needless
to say, comical; and Alphonso Spagoni, the villain of Billy
Merson's song, is no exception. Yet it is Billy himself who was
humiliated. Alphonso is a matador, whose 'daring display'
Billy and his girl watch in the arena. But 'while I'd gone out
for some nuts and a programme, The dirty dog stole her
away'. The tune is a lively pastiche on bullring music, rising
to a treble climax when Merson swears to 'raise a bunion on
his Spanish onion'. What is taken completely for granted in
this number—as in so many—is that Billy's girl *would* immediately desert him for the dazzling matador. For if there are
endless laments by girl singers about the faithlessness of their
swains, the men are just as certain girls are fickle. Another

quality of this song, as in all the best ones, is how aptly the words match the music, the one always a pointed commentary on the other. Indeed, it's often the music rather than the lyric that makes the point—in this case to convey the extravagant glamour of the matador, and the dejection and discomfiture of the singer.

At this point we may already notice that, even in the serious songs, the concept of tragic love is completely absent from the Music Hall canon: it is never Romeo and Juliet who are involved, but either Touchstone and Audrey or, at best, Rosalind and Orlando. This is at first surprising, for if one considers contemporary French, German or Spanish popular numbers, the tragic possibilities of the grand passion are constantly exploited. Yvette Guilbert, for example, though she sang many light-hearted ditties satirizing love, could also pull out all the stops and give her audiences a vision of love culminating in real, not comical, disaster. Indeed, while tragic themes in general are favourite material for such singer-bards as Aristide Bruant, and while the witty and scandalous Yvette could also transform herself, in certain numbers, into a harlot, murderess, or suicidal *femme fatale*, in the Music Hall canon there is hardly a whisper of all this.

Nor, even, is the sexual element in love lyrics fully exploited. In the comic numbers, there is certainly much scarcely disguised innuendo: yet the notion that the animal element in love is not only ludicrous, but also vital to it, is quite absent. It is this almost total lack of tragedy in the Music Hall songs that makes the English canon, despite its enormous charms, inferior—or, at any rate, less rich—to those of continental countries. I once tried to write a Music Hall play in which the actual songs were to be used; but found the chief difficulty was that since the songs are so devoid of drama, it was almost impossible to devise dramatic situations that these songs could illustrate.

But why is this? Surely there were heartbreaks and dramas enough in Victorian and Edwardian working-class life? Then why did the audiences not want to hear of them, and the singers and composers instinctively know this? One may, of course, put this down to English reticence, but perhaps another reason is that working class audiences of those days knew enough tragedy in their real lives not to want to see it demonstrated on the stage. But French popular audiences surely knew plenty about disaster too, yet enjoyed the release a portrayal of it by a singer could afford them. Yet English Music Hall songs, so frank and realistic on less vital levels, consistently skate over any cracks in the surface of life that are really disturbing.

This was not always quite so, apparently. In the infancy of the Halls, in the 1850s and 60s, W G Ross sang, at the Cyder Cellars, a number which, in an indecent army version, still survives in barrack-rooms. This was *Sam Hall*, which opens with

> My name is Sam Hall, chimney sweep.
> My name is Sam Hall,
> I robs both great and small,
> But they make me pay for all—
> Damn their eyes.

Ross played this as a condemned criminal—a figure one never meets later in the century, unless it be a 'comic' villain like those of Billy Bennett's. By the 'seventies, even Ross had graduated to more respectable panto; and other primitives were already exploiting the comic—albeit frank and realistic —aspects of London life. Frederick Robson (1821–1864), known in his day as 'the greatest genius since Edmund Kean', launched the immortal *Villikins and his Dinah*. Sam Cowell (1819–1864) took over the number and added to his repertory the equally illustrious *Rat-catcher's Daughter*. Sam Collins (1826–1865—the Hall in Islington, recently demolished, was named after him) sang comic Irish numbers like *Paddy's Wedding*. Most of these are indeed songs that have an intimate naturalism greater than in those of most later Cockney singers. But even so, tragedy remains hidden. The only two sorts of 'realism' popular audiences accepted were that of

LOVE

the melodramas—*Maria Marten, Sweeney Todd* and so on—which survived (though played in a somewhat camped-up, satirical style) in the performances of Tod Slaughter that could still be seen as late as the 1940s; or else the muted realism of the Music Halls.

It is a dogma of male singers of the satirical love numbers that the woman is the pursuer, not the pursued, and that usually older than the man, she is out to get him by hook or, more usually, crook. One of Harry Champion's best numbers, *I'm Henery the Eighth, I am* illustrated this belief. As well as this song, Harry Champion launched two other Music Hall perennials, *Boiled Beef and Carrots* and *Any Old Iron?*, and each of these songs has in common that they are boisterous and enthusiastic rather than sardonic, as if whatever happens to anyone—however ludicrous or otherwise disastrous—is immensely funny. The thought of a singer bouncing on the stage to demonstrate his absolute conviction that life is one long hearty laugh, may repel the sensitive reader, but I can only assure him that Harry Champion made this supposition entirely convincing. He shot on from the wings as if projected by a missile and, with an enormous grin on his broad rubicund face, battered out his numbers like an amiable machine gun. I saw him once striding about singing in front of a drop cloth representing a street, into which he accidentally backed so that he fell into the tottering cloth in a semi-sitting position whence he was unable to rise. Not a whit disconcerted, he went on belting out his number from this recumbent posture until an invisible stage hand heaved him to his feet from behind the drop. On another occasion, when well on in his seventies (he was reticent about the date of his birth, but he made his début around 1888, and died in 1942), he sang, in a revival at the Palladium, his cherished *Boiled Beef and Carrots*. The first line of the opening verse of this runs

Now, when I was a nipper not six months old . . .

The thought of his being of this age struck Harry as so vastly

41

comical that he exploded, with the audience, into hysterics, and had to make several false starts before he could get into the number.

Henry VIII is, of course, an English popular hero—among monarchs, the only one the bare mention of whose name is always good for a laugh. *I'm Henery the Eighth, I am,* in which Champion becomes his latter-day namesake, has the additional comic twist that it is the Widow Burch, not Harry, who's already been married so often. Incidentally, although it is generally supposed that the English masses revere the monarchy, this immensely popular ditty may suggest that their real attitude is somewhat different. It's by Murray and Weston, a team who composed jointly, and who never revealed their first names on the song-sheets.

You don't know who you're looking at; now take a look at
    me!
I'm a bit of a nob, I am—belong to royaltee.
I'll tell you how it came about; I married Widow Burch,
And I was the King of England when I trotted out to church.
Outside the people started shouting, 'Hip—hooray!'
Said I, 'Get down upon your knees, it's Coronation Day!

    I'm Henery the Eighth, I am!
    Henery the Eighth, I am, I am!
    I got married to the widow next door,
    She's been married seven times before.
    Ev'ry one was a Henery—
    She wouldn't have a Willie or a Sam.
    I'm her eighth old man named Henery,
    Henery the Eighth I am!'

The most memorable misfortune that took place at the altar is, of course, recorded in Vesta Victoria's *Waiting at the Church* (music by Henry E Pether, lyrics by Fred W Leigh). Occasionally, Vesta sang 'straight' numbers, as her exceedingly pretty *All in a day,* which we shall be meeting later on. But her habitual role was that of the innocent, dopey girl on whom fate played the cruellest tricks—but who never, never despaired. Hope sprang eternal in her yearning breast.

Vesta Victoria exploited this situation in her songs for all it was worth. In *Waiting at the Church*, for instance, her young man sends her a note to say, 'Can't get away to marry you today—My wife won't let me!' ('Lord, how it did upset me!' is Vesta's comment). In *Poor John!* (by the same lyric writer and composer), she dwells painfully on the mother-in-law and daughter-in-law situation. On her first visit to her young man's mother,

> She put me through a cross-examination;
> I fairly boiled with aggravation.
> Then she shook her head, looked at me and said,
> 'Poor John! Poor John!'

In *Now I have to call him father* (by Chas Collins and Fred Godfrey jointly) her treacherous young man marries her mother behind her back. Though here one might notice, in passing, that although Vesta Victoria had these numbers, songs about mothers-in-law in the Halls were by no means so frequent as popular legend might suggest. Many who do not know the vast variety of themes they dealt with seem to imagine this was the only Music Hall jest.

Even more than Marie Lloyd, Vesta Victoria was a past-mistress at innuendo. With an air of totally bland innocence, she would deliver apparently innocuous lines, her chaste eyes failing to understand what the audience found so funny. For instance, in *Poor John!*, when she is describing her courting, she declares in the most tender and factual way,

> He took me out for walks, and oh! he was so nice!
> He always used to kiss me on the same place twice.

A song of hers that is loaded with double meanings is her celebrated *Daddy wouldn't buy me a bow-wow* (words and music by Joseph Tabrar) in which she laments that

Daddy wouldn't buy me a bow-wow (bow-wow),
Daddy wouldn't buy me a bow-wow (bow-wow),
I've got a little cat
And I'm very fond of that,
But I'd rather have a bow-wow-wow.

Who was Daddy? He was, in fact, the sugar daddy, later to
be celebrated in the transatlantic number, *My heart belongs to
daddy*. As for the 'little cat' she was so fond of, and the 'bow-
wow-wow' she would have preferred, what these really were
could—despite Vesta's decorous, appealing tone—be left to
the audience's imagination.

I saw her once appear as a bedraggled wife carrying
pathetically a battered kettle. With a look of earnest appeal
for the audience's considerate sympathy, she told us that

My old man has been and run away from me—
He's taken everything with him I do declare,
The three-legged table and the old arm chair.
All he's left is this kettle and it's all worn out . . .
Now what's the use of an old tin kettle to a woman if it hasn't
    got a spout?

George Beauchamp (1863–1901) launched, in an earlier
generation, another famous song of total defeat in which
'Mabel the fair pulled out my hair, And clawed all the skin
off my nose'. This was *She was one of the Early Birds (And I
was one of the Worms)*—words and music by T W Connor.
Once again, the financial aspect of marriage as the chief cause
of its undoing is underlined:

> She was a dear little dicky bird,
> 'Chip, chip, chip,' she went,
> Sweetly she sang to me
> Till all my money was spent;
> Then she went off song—
> We parted on fighting terms,
> She was one of the early birds,
> And I was one of the worms.

44

LOVE

Even more gloomy is Tom Costello's *At Trinity Church I met my Doom* with music and lyrics by Fred Gilbert. The first verse sails straight into the theme:

> Twelve months ago with decent chances,
> Prospects of success in life,
> Through foolish love of ballroom dances,
> Trouble came—I met my wife.

And in the chorus, money ('Up to my eyes in debt for "renty"') again appears as the chief source of disillusionment. Tom Costello (1863–1943) specialized, however, in manly 'heroic' numbers like *Comrades, The Ship I Love,* or *I've made up my mind to sail away,* which we shall be meeting later. This last (words and music by Bennett Scott) was one of the many songs of the period about emigration to what were then called (even in the cases of such places as Australia and Canada) 'the colonies': indeed, for a male singer, in any dire misfortune this instantly occurred as a solution—as it no doubt did in reality to many young men in his audience. Fred Barnes, for instance, in *Black Sheep of the Family* (words and music by Fred Davis) affirms that 'I'll go out to the colonies, And there I'll rise or fall . . . And when I come back, The sheep that was black Will perhaps be the whitest sheep of all'. 'Perhaps'—for many singers confessed that the colonies claimed them forever, as we shall hear in Leo Dryden's *The Miner's dream of Home.*

Tom Costello's 'heroic' numbers would be exceedingly difficult to sing today with any conviction—though the old boy himself manages them splendidly, as an excellent electrical recording, made in his old age, bears witness. And when we come to the songs in the section *Soldiers and Sailors* many readers will, I think, wonder how on earth the singers ever got away with them. I shall try to explain later on why I think this was possible, but one reason may already be apparent—which is the robust conviction with which the Music Hall artists could project songs of almost ludicrous optimism. This was no doubt in part because, before World War I, although material life was unquestionably much harder than it is today, the popular psychological mood was much more relaxed. The social order, however oppressive to the majority, seemed enormously stable, and this I think accounts for the stalwart buoyancy of the Music Hall singers—however pathetic, and indeed unreal, we may find this spirit to be in the light of our later knowledge of all that was to overtake English society after 1914.

There is also, undoubtedly, in these songs—and even more, in the delivery of them—a marked and vehement virility. Of course, it is a strength that survived because it left so much out, but nevertheless it is formidably there. Thus, while we may find it hard to concede—as Orwell has pointed out —that our grandfathers were better men than we are, I don't think there's much doubt that English men and women (of all classes) were more robust then than they are now. We may be wiser (though even that, perhaps, is doubtful), and we're certainly more disillusioned; but it may be doubted if, despite our greater (though I think very relative) social equality and material wealth, we are in fact happier. If this seems a reactionary statement, then I can only say that the whole tone of these songs and singers—their conviction, and their gusto, and their manifest faith—does powerfully suggest that those vanished generations enjoyed themselves more than ours do, even though we may find the sources of their enjoyment crude and over-simplified, and their ignorance about so much of themselves enormous.

Another reflection at this stage is what an astonishingly sharp instinct popular audiences then had for picking winners. Of course, there were doubtless hundreds of inferior artists who were greatly admired, and who are now completely forgotten. It must also be conceded that certain popular favourites—as G H Chirgwin, whom we shall be meeting later—seem, from all that one can learn about them, to have been, as artists, quite appalling. Nor can it be denied that today as well, the pop public has a sure instinct to pick out, with amazing rapidity, the best of the current favourites. But the difference between now and then seems to me to be this. Today, there is a vast propaganda apparatus to guide—or seek to influence—the public in its choice: the current pop stars are projected on LPs, television, radio and the screen, and extensively reviewed in newspapers and magazines targeted at all classes. In the Music Hall era, the means of publicity were primitive, and before gramophone recording (which, as I have explained, came too late and was too little used to influence the public greatly), the fans could only get to know about the latest stars either by trudging to the local Music Hall to see them in the flesh, or by getting hold of the sheet music of their songs if somebody in the family could play the piano. They were helped in their choice to some extent by notes in the popular press, it is true; but there was nothing like the organized criticism of today, and among educated writers, only mavericks like Shaw and Beerbohm noticed the Halls at all.

Yet despite what seem to have been considerable obstacles, the proletarian public not only rallied to the best artists with remarkable speed, but also got, on the whole, their priorities extraordinarily right. There may have been differences of opinion about minor stars, but everyone knew that Marie Lloyd was a greater artist than Vesta Victoria (however much they may have admired Vesta), Little Tich a finer comic than T E Dunville, or Dan Leno a profounder clown than Wilkie Bard. This was proved in the most practical way by the higher fees these greater artists could command. I think (if I may be so dreary as to draw a moral) there is a 'lesson' in this for any 'educated' person who confronts any popular art form: which is that popular taste, which can indeed in some of its manifestations ardently pursue the deplorable, has also an astonishing resiliency in spotting and supporting talented artists—and this, so often, long before the 'educated' persons have even heard of them.

London Life

ALTHOUGH Music Hall soon spread from London to the provinces, and although provincial (and Irish and Scottish) artists were soon to become stars, the whole art began in London, and the bulk of the greatest artists remained Londoners.

The 'music halls' began round about the 1840s simply as adjuncts to public houses when the landlords discovered that a song encouraged customers to drink. These rapidly grew in size—the 'hall' becoming larger than the adjoining pub itself —but until the 'seventies and 'eighties, most Music Halls remained attached to a local tavern. In those days the audience sat not in rows of seats, but at chairs beside tables where drink and food (pease puddings and pigs' trotters were favourite dishes) were sold by waiters like 'Brush' Wood, Marie Lloyd's father. The entertainment was presided over by a Chairman, a man of voluble authority and strong local popularity, who sat at a table at the foot of the stage, introduced the numbers, rebuked interrupters, encouraged further orders from the waiters, and courteously accepted drinks from admiring clients. The Chairman called for order with a hammer, and also used this, after his preparatory spiel ('Ladies and gentlemen, I give you the one and only etc etc'), to assure a rousing reception to each new artist.

Throughout the 'eighties and 'nineties, larger Halls were built as theatres proper, and the Chairmen, presiding over a smaller gathering of some two to three hundred people, gradually disappeared, though Chairmen were still functioning in the 'nineties at Gatti's, Westminster bridge, and Collins' in Islington. The most legendary of the early Music Hall impresarios was Charles Morton, who built the Palace (still standing) in the 'nineties. He'd begun at the Canterbury Arms in Westminster Bridge road which he started in 1849, and in addition to Music Hall turns, he'd put on opera and exhibitions of painting so that his theatre became known as the 'Academy over the water'. He rose as the Halls did, launching, as we shall soon see, many new talents, and by the time he built the Palace in Shaftesbury avenue, was a figure of some substance in the theatrical and even social world. Seeing a well-dressed client stub out his cigar on the sumptuous carpet of his new theatre, he told the man to leave: 'I would not do that in your house, sir. You shall not do it in mine.' Many of the new theatres became known as Palaces of Variety, and an attempt was made by theatrical entrepreneurs to attract a wider, less proletarian public, and to enforce seemly behaviour inside the Halls. The wire netting stretched over the orchestra pit to protect the musicians from missiles hurled from the gallery at the performers was no longer deemed necessary, nor were the bottles still chained, as they used to be, to the waiters' trays. The 'Gallery Boys' were tamed, if not altogether subdued, though in the North they continued to fling iron rivets at inept performers.

Those who can remember the Queen's Poplar, or the Metropolitan Edgware road, could form an idea of what the hundreds of smaller local Halls were like. In both of these Halls, there was the agreeable architectural situation that you could watch the show through a wide glass panel from the inside of the main stalls bar—indeed, the Queen's later wired this for sound, so that there was no need to leave the bar at all if you didn't want to. The Metropolitan, like the Bedford Camden Town both of which Sickert frequented and recorded—were exceedingly pretty, being adorned with ornate statuary in a pop art rococo that has now completely vanished. As for the Granville Walham Green, it was tiled throughout in decorated faïence, so that one had rather the impression of being in a vast swimming pool.

Towards the turn of the century, big theatrical business moved into the Halls, in the persons, principally, of Oswald Stoll and Maurice de Freece (who became the husband of

Vesta Tilley, of whom more later). The old single-act programmes running without a break from 6.30 p m to midnight
were replaced by 'twice nightly' performances—one of the
many causes of the Music Hall strike of 1907 in which the
artists, led by Marie Lloyd—and to the immense delight of
the populace—picketed the chief theatres in central London.
Stoll built Empires throughout the provinces, and joining
with Moss, founded Moss Empires who erected vast palaces
like the Hippodrome (now Talk of the Town) and the Coliseum.
In these huge barns intimacy and direct contact with the
audience were of course impossible, and though the stars
grew even richer (as did their promoters), the art was already
in decline.

Perhaps the most famous London Hall was the Old Mogul,
or Old Mo, in Drury Lane. Originally the Old Mogul tavern,
this started as a modest Hall, was rebuilt more lavishly in
1872, and in 1891 was once again re-furbished and transformed
more decorously into the Middlesex. With the fading of the
Halls it underwent a further metamorphosis into the Winter
Garden theatre, and as such lingered on until quite recently.
A playbill of a gala evening at the Middlesex on 20th March,
1902, in honour of 'the Popular and Only Marie Lloyd', shows
that no less than one hundred and four turns appeared (at
prices ranging from sixpence to five shillings), and among
them more than a dozen stars. Also advertised on this bill
was the 'Edisonograph', more usually known as the 'bioscope'
—a gadget which was shown at the end of the programme,
when everyone was getting up to leave; for few foresaw that
the 'Edisonograph' would, within two decades, invade almost
all of the old Halls and expel the live artists entirely.

Down the road from the Old Mo (or Middlesex) there stood,
of course, the Theatre Royal Drury Lane. And in the late
'eighties this came under the management of Sir Augustus
('Druriolanus') Harris, whose tenancy is commemorated by a
portrait bust at the entrance to the theatre, where he now
stares at patrons of *Hello Dolly* (or whatever it may be) with
a contorted expression remarkably resembling that of Edward

VII—whom, indeed, so many eminent men at the turn of the century contrived to look like. In the late 'eighties, Harris hit upon the brilliant plan of reviving the pantomimes so popular in Grimaldi's day and, to give them a contemporary twist and attract multitudinous clients, to invite selected stars from the Halls to take part. This invitation came as something of a surprise to the Music Hall artists who thought the Lane altogether too grand for them, yet they accepted. Accordingly, some of the greatest stars migrated from the Halls to the Lane at Christmas time, and Dan Leno, Little Tich, Marie Lloyd, Vesta Tilley, Herbert Campbell, Johnny Danvers, Harry Randall and Harry Fragson all appeared there. I shall describe Drury Lane pantos when we come to Dan Leno, but meanwhile would mention that Harry Fragson, like Little Tich, was one of the rare English artists who was as popular in Paris as in London. Song sheets of the 'Répertoire Fragson' appeared in France throughout the Edwardian era, and Fragson's Cockney accent when speaking French in Paris was apparently as hilarious as his device of speaking English with a Parisian accent when in London.

The pick of the Music Hall artists thus became known to a much wider public, since Drury Lane pantos were considered, unlike the Halls, to be suitable entertainment for the young. 'Serious' theatrical critics also began to devote space to their activities, though their comments were usually condescending, and frequently disapproving. Thus, Mr William Archer on Marie Lloyd and Dan Leno in the 'bedroom scene' of *Robinson Crusoe*:

> You may think it odd, and even ungallant, but somehow I don't seem to yearn for the privilege of assisting at Miss Marie Lloyd's toilet, or admiring Mr Dan Leno in déshabille; but amid all that vast audience, I was evidently in a minority of one.

At the Lane was also perfected that theatrical absurdity, the English pantomime, which bore but little relation to its Italian origins, and which still lingers on today in the provinces and suburbs. For pretty girls to play Principal Boys, and ugly men Dames (or as Leno did, a Baroness, Sister Anne, and Mother Goose), was, of course, just up the alley of the Music Hall artists for, as we shall see, impersonation of male artists by women, and vice versa, was a commonplace on the Halls.

For our emblematic artist of the London scene, we must once again choose Gus Elen. He had a number devoted specifically to this theme, *The Cove wot's lived in London all 'is Life*, and three finer songs describe London indirectly—*Down the Road, 'E Dunno where 'E Are*, and *If it wasn't for the 'ouses in between*. In *Down the Road* (words and music by Fred Gilbert), Gus, as a coster, matches his mare Polly against Tom Jones the butcher's cob for a wager of 'fifty bright sovrins' —quite a lot, one might have thought, even for a prosperous coster. Polly wins the race and the bet for Gus, but . . . he kills her in the process. And though he declares, 'And grief too keen to talk about was mine', he doesn't seem all that upset about it. Might this suggest that the popular attitude to animals (especially when a prize of £50 was involved) was not so tender as among the middle classes, who didn't use them for their work?

Like many titles of Music Hall numbers, *'E Dunno where 'E Are* (music Fred Eplett, lyrics Harry Wright) has an epigrammatic ring. The theme here is that of a working-class man who steps out of line, and is unfaithful to the sense of solidarity with his former mates. Here are the first verse and chorus:

Jack Jones is well known to ev'rybody
Round about the market, don't yer see,
I've no fault to find wiv Jack at all
When 'e's as 'e used ter be,
But some'ow since 'e's 'ad the bullion left
'E's altered for the wust,
When I sees the way 'e treats old pals
I am filled wiv nuffing but disgust.

52

LONDON LIFE

'E says as 'ow we isn't class enuf,
Sez we ain't upon a par
Wiv 'im just because 'e's better off—
Won't smoke a pipe, must take on a cigar . . .

When 'e's up at Covent Garden you can see 'im standin' all
    alone,
Won't join in a quiet Tommy Dodd,
Drinkin' Scotch and Soda on 'is own.
'As the cheek and impidence to call 'is muvver 'is ma,
Since Jack Jones come into a little bit o' splosh,
Why 'e don't know where 'e are.

Once again, we may see here the recurring inheritance myth
. . . and we may also notice what Gus regards as disloyal
behaviour on the enriched Jones's part. His chief crime, of
course, is that he's 'standing all alone'—if he'd stood everybody a drink instead, there would probably have been no
objection (nor, of course, any song). Scotch and soda, let
alone a cigar, are evidently the height of pretension . . . and
this feeling seems to survive, for I noticed, when in the army,
that lads who spent fortunes on beer and fags regarded
either of these more classy indulgences (except, perhaps, on
birthdays or at Christmas) as highly suspect. Until I heard
this song, I had always imagined Cockneys *did* say 'Ma'—but
evidently this was petty bourgeois, and 'muvver' is—or was
—correct. The 'Tommy Dodd' Jack won't join in is rhyming
slang for 'even and odd', and denotes a gambling game. (In a
later verse, one of Jack Jones's enormities is to read the
'Telegraft' instead of, presumably, *Lloyd's Weekly*.)

If it wasn't for the 'ouses in between is yet another idyll that
betrays the coster's (somewhat theoretical) nostalgia for the
country, and his determination, at all costs, to have a garden
of some kind even in the smallest of back yards—an instinct
which, in east and south London, still more or less survives.
The tune is by George Le Brunn and the lyric by Edgar
Bateman—one of the Music Hall's happiest teams, whom we

have already met in Elen's *It's a great big shame*. It is, I think, one of the most perfect of the Music Hall ditties in that it has a delightful blend of matter-of-fact realism coupled with mildly ironical lyricism:

If you saw my little back yard, 'Wot a pretty spot!' you'd
    cry—
It's a picture on a sunny summer day;
Wiv the turnip tops and cabbages wot people doesn't buy
I makes it on a Sunday look all gay.
The neighbours finks I grows 'em and you'd fancy you're in
    Kent,
Or at Epsom if you gaze into the mews—
It's a wonder as the landlord doesn't want to raise the rent,
Because we've got such nobby distant views.

Oh! it really is a werry pretty garden,
And Chingford to the eastward could be seen;
Wiv a ladder and some glasses,
You could see to 'Ackney marshes,
If it wasn't for the 'ouses in between.

Notice how the rent crops up yet again, even in the midst of this little idyll! Elen can't get lyrical, as in his *You could almost shut your eyes and 'ear 'em grow* as well, without striking a note of relevant bathos.

George Orwell once wrote that he'd rather have written some of the Music Hall songs than a great many poems in the anthologies (the example he envied was *Come where the booze is cheaper—come where the pots hold more*). Perhaps, if he had been a poet, he would not have said this—yet I do not think it can be denied that Edgar Bateman is a highly accomplished versifier . . . it all looks so easy, yet the more one examines it, the more adroit the whole thing appears. It is also in perfect harmony with the melody . . . and I do wish the reader could hear this—and so many other tunes —since the Music Hall lyrics were all created directly as songs, and never as poems later to be 'set to music'. Incidentally, in subsequent verses Edgar Bateman has no difficulty whatever in ringing the changes on the telling absurdity of the last three lines—the supposition that if the ''ouses in between' weren't there (which, in London, they so manifestly were), the prospect of the world at large would be sensational. Thus:

> If I got a rope and pulley
> I'd enjoy the breeze more fully . . .

Or

> If you climbed up on a chimbley
> You could see right out to Wembley . . .

Or even

> If yer eyesight didn't fail yer
> Yer could see right to Australia . . .

Another quality in this and other songs the reader will surely already have noticed is that almost without exception, they describe recognizable characters in clearly-defined situations. This is one great difference, I think, between Music Hall songs and pop numbers of today; and in this sense, Music Hall songs seem to me superior. Most modern pops are synthetic: they describe—or rather, evoke—an imprecise, glamourized view of life, and one rarely exactly knows who the persons the performer sings about may actually be, or where they live, or much about what they do. Of course, this is in one sense their whole point—their very impersonality. Nor am I denying that some modern pops, in their abstract way, are better than others. But this does mean that almost everything (so far as the lyric goes) depends on the delivery. In the Music Hall numbers, the best lyrics can stand up by themselves, even divorced from their singer and their tune.

In Harry Champion's *Any Old Iron?* (music by Chas Collins, lyric by Fred Terry and A E Sheppard), we once again encounter the wishful thought, or fantasy, of an inheritance. The song is not—as its title might at first suggest—about a rag-and-bone man collecting scrap metal. No, the 'old iron' in question is the 'gold' watch and chain his Uncle Bill left him when he 'went and kicked the bucket', which turns out to be of baser metal; and when Harry's mates discover this, they mock him. This song would suggest that though the 'inheritance' fantasy was widespread, it wasn't perhaps taken all that seriously. Harry's attitude to his uncle's death, by the way, is very straightforward: no tears whatever are shed for Uncle Bill. This is a long way removed from the morbidities of the Minstrel numbers that I mentioned earlier. It is a rattling rhyme, and perhaps of all Harry's songs the best suited to his staccato delivery. This is the chorus; a 'tile' is, of course, a hat:

Any old iron—any old iron—
Any any old, old iron?
You look neat—talk about a treat—
You look dapper from your napper to your feet
Dress'd in style, brand new tile,
And your father's old green tie on,
But I wouldn't give you tuppence for your old watch chain,
Old iron—old iron?

And what of the London matriarchs—the wives of the stalwart, laconic men that we've been meeting? They certainly match up to their husbands in their realism: their attitude to their better halves is entirely disillusioned . . . and yet entirely faithful. However dreadful the old man may be—and he often is—the old girl is loyal to the core. Orwell,[1] yet again, has pointed out the essentially moral view that the English working classes have—or had—of marriage, and the Music Hall songs bear this out. Of course, temptation to the wife is frankly admitted—the milkman and the lodger

---

[1] Though Orwell often refers to Music Hall songs, and certainly knew the Halls, so far as I know he didn't write about them. This seems an enormous pity, for surely they would have provided him with an even richer theme than boys' magazines and comic post cards.

are the Music Hall Don Juans, and Wilkie Bard had a bitter
number called *Never 'ave a lodger for a pal* (though Vesta
Victoria countered this with *Our lodger's such a nice young
man*). Likewise, the supposition that the husband is a
philanderer—or wants to be one—is an enduring convention.
All the same, the basic assumption about marriage is that
however much the man and wife may want to kick over the
traces, when it comes to the point, they stick it out, as best
they can, in the strait and narrow path of conjugal fidelity.
How true this really was to life it is of course impossible to
know, yet even if a myth does not correspond to a reality, it
denotes a presupposition of what this reality should be.

In Marie Lloyd's most famous 'character' number, *My old
man says, 'Follow the van'* (music by Chas Collins, lyric by
Fred W Leigh), we shall thus notice that though Marie goes
astray, her homing instinct doesn't fail her. The theme of this
number is a recurrent one—the 'midnight flit', or 'shooting
the moon', when you moved out of the house by night before
the broker's men had time to move in. The theme, indeed,
pops up so frequently in Music Hall numbers that one may
guess it was a familiar experience to many of the audience
—and no doubt to some of the singers who came, almost
without exception, from poor families. One can thus immediately see yet another difficulty—that is, apart from aesthetic
interpretation—for any modern performers who want to sing
these songs: they just haven't had the personal experience
so many of the songs arise from, nor have modern audiences.
A song about a 'midnight flit', sung today, would thus seem
to most of the audience merely titillating, and would not
touch them on any wry, personal nerve of comic anxiety.

The economy with which Fred W Leigh establishes his
whole theme in the six opening lines of the first verse is
admirable:

> We had to move away
> 'Cos the rent we couldn't pay,
> The moving van came round just after dark;

There was me and my old man
Shoving things inside the van,
Which we'd often done before, let me remark . . .

Since there is no room for Marie (or her pet bird, after whom
the number is sometimes called 'The Cock-linnet song'), she
explains what happens in the chorus:

My old man said, 'Follow the van,
Don't dilly dally on the way!'
Off went the cart with the home packed in it,
I walked behind with my old cock linnet.
But I dillied and dallied, dallied and dillied,
Lost the van and don't know where to roam . . .
I stopped on the way to have the old half quartern,
And I can't find my way home.

In a song of Lily Morris's, by Harry Castling (music) and
James Welsh (lyric), called *Don't have any more, Mrs Moore*,
the character and situation are put before the audience with
the same admirable brevity. Lily's Mrs Moore wanted more
of everything—husbands, children and liquor—despite Lily's
warning, so far as the latter went, that 'Too many double
gins Give the ladies double chins'. The technique is unusual,
in that Lily Morris is describing—like a sort of Cockney chorus
—what Mrs Moore is up to, without our ever hearing from
that robust old girl herself. But by the time Lily had finished
—or even as soon as she began the song—the deplorable, if
absent, Mrs Moore was fully visible to the audience.

Misses Moore, who lives next door,
She's such a dear old soul.
Of children she's a score or more,
Her husband's on the dole.
I don't know how she manages to keep that lot, I'm sure;
I said to her today as she was standing by the door:

'Don't have any more, Misses Moore,
Misses Moore, please don't have any more.
The more you have, the more you'll want, they say,
But enough is as good as a feast any day.
If you have any more, Misses Moore,
You'll have to rent the house next door . . .
Oh! they're all right when they're here,
But take my advice, old dear—
Don't have any more, Misses Moore.'

Something of an exception to the convention that Music
Hall songs are never tragic, is Ella Shields's *Burlington Bertie
from Bow*. This was written to words and music by William
Hargreaves, whom she married not long after she arrived in
England from the United States. It is curious to reflect that
this most 'Cockney' of numbers was, like Gene Stratton's
Lily of Laguna, sung by an American: the more so as, even
in old age, Ella Shields's accent was still quite recognizable.
Born in 1879, she first came over in Edwardian days as
what was then known as a 'coon shouter'—that is, a white
artist who purported to sing Negro songs in the new ragtime
style.

The title of her famous song is rather confusing, since
Hargreaves is in fact commenting, in his number, on another
Burlington Bertie who preceded Ella's one from Bow. This
was a creation of Vesta Tilley's (of whom more soon), and her
Bertie was a masher, a toff, a knut, of whom Vesta sang,
'I'm Burlington Bertie, I rise at ten-thirty, and toddle along
to the Strand.' But in Hargreaves' version for Ella, Bertie
has fallen on evil days, migrated to Bow, and is vainly trying
to recapture his past glories: he's down, but he's by no means
out. The impact of the song, when Ella Shields first sang it,
must have been due to the knowledge among the audience
that in those days you were either very rich or poor; that
there was an enormous gulf between the classes, it was
extremely hard to climb from one to another, and if you
fell, you fell hard. The tune has a somewhat sinister ring,

highly unusual in the canon; and an excellent electrical recording of it still survives.

I'm Bert . . . p'r'aps you've heard of me,
Bert . . . you've had word of me,
Jogging along, hearty and strong, living on plates of fresh air.
I dress up in fashion, and when I am feeling depressed,
I shave from my cuff all the whiskers and fluff, stick my hat
    on and toodle up West.

I'm Burlington Bertie,
I rise at ten-thirty, and saunter along like a toff,
I walk down the Strand with my gloves on my hand,
Then I walk down again with them off.
I'm all airs and graces, correct easy paces,
Without food so long I've forgot where my face is—
I'm Bert, Bert, I haven't a shirt, but my people are well off,
    you know!
Nearly ev'ryone knows me, from Smith to Lord Roseb'ry,
I'm Burlington Bertie from Bow!

The tale goes on for several verses, growing increasingly harrowing. Ella Shields used to sing it prowling about the stage, and even as late as the 1940s, the audience seemed to get rather uneasy. The whole thing was performed in male attire, which she carried off most convincingly. For Ella was one of the three great 'male impersonators'—the others being Vesta Tilley and Hetty King—and of this style I shall say more when we come to consider Vesta. It may be noticed, by the way, how often the Strand crops up in Music Hall songs as the most glamorous street in London. One wouldn't think so of that woebegone thoroughfare today, but in Ella's time, of course, it was graced by the Tivoli, the most famous of the smaller Halls, by the Gaiety at the east end of it, and by the chief theatrical restaurant, Romano's. (I haven't been able to identify the 'Smith' she refers to as a personage as illustrious as Lord Roseb'ry. Evidently it was too early for F E. Or is she perhaps being ironical in juxtaposing an aristocratic name with a common one? Can anyone help?)

I saw a lot of Ella Shields before her death, and unlike most Music Hall artists I have met, she was a bit of an intellectual, and liked analysing her art; whereas most of the artists shut up like clams if you tried to get them off any subject but their own past triumphs always voluminously, if not so accurately, described. Ella revealed to me that characteristic blend of toughness, even hardness, and of gushing sentiment that seemed characteristic of so many Music Hall stars. Of other artists, especially younger ones, she often spoke with extreme, and I thought rather bitchy, severity. But she could also dissolve into effusive recollection. The dressing-room at the Tivoli, she told me, was so small that the stars had to make up among the minor artists in the same room, and in these circumstances she first met Marie Lloyd:

> And I stood with my ears and mouth open to look at her. And I remember what she said. 'So you're the great coon shouter. You don't look like a coon shouter. You know what you look like? You look like a dainty Maid of Albion.' And I must confess my ignorance—I didn't know what the word Albion meant. And it shows you the loveliness of the woman—in her nature. I was the newcomer and stranger among them, and she said: 'Why, you're just a blooming lovely English girl!'

On one occasion she took me for a drink at a dreadful haunt near the B B C, now transformed, called the Bolivar. I suggested Scotch, but she insisted on a bottle of champagne, and paid for it with a fiver. Evidently she was one of the artists who, unlike Marie Lloyd, were savers, and she carried all this off (though aged then in her seventies) with Edwardian aplomb.

Americans are not the only artists who invaded the English Halls: there were also three famous Australians: Billy Williams, 1877–1915; Albert Whelan (born 1875 and died not long ago) who is said to have invented the 'signature tune', for he always came on stage whistling *Der Lüstige Brüder*; and Florrie Forde, born in 1876, who became, thanks to a famous song of World War I, a Music Hall immortal. All three hailed from Melbourne, and knowing that grim city all too well, it astonishes me that it should have had such illustrious sons and daughters. The Aussie accent is quite apparent in Florrie's songs, many of which survive in electrical recordings. Bud Flanagan, by the way, one of the last artists to carry the Music Hall spirit into our own era, used to play in Florrie's troupe in his younger days.

Florrie Forde's two perennials are *Pack up your troubles in your old kit bag* and *Down at the old Bull and Bush*. We shall be hearing more of wartime songs in the section on *Soldiers and Sailors*, but meanwhile can salute with moderation the *Bull and Bush* number as one that is usually considered a typical Cockney number. In point of fact, it isn't. For not only was Florrie not a Cockney (despite her being billed as 'The Australian Marie Lloyd'), but the coster migrations to Hampstead Heath were already in decline when Florrie made the song popular, and the pub there (rebuilt but still surviving) had become more of a petty bourgeois haunt. It is a brash, raucous song, with music by Harry von Tilzer and no less than three librettists—Andrew B Stirling, Russell Hunting and Percy Krone. Personally, I have always found it, with its forced jollity and demure 'Just let me hold your hand, dear' mildly revolting, though there is no doubt Florrie bashed it out with considerable effect.

Those who remember George Formby, of the ukelele and the toothy grin, may not know that his father, George Formby Senior was, in his day, an equally renowned artist. He was one of the earliest great Music Hall performers from the provinces, and when he appeared in London, no doubt to assuage the feelings of the contemptuous Cockneys, he devised a character called 'John Willie from Lancashire' who embodied the gormless, guileless Lancashire lad adrift in the wicked capital. The titles of some of his numbers will convey the tone: *I'm such a hit with the girls, Since I parted my hair in the middle, All of a sudden it struck me,* and *John Willie, come on!* My own favourite is *Playing the game in the West* by Alec Kendall and George himself) in which Formby sets out to paint the capital red. It was sung in a reedy, defiant, amiable squeak.

Since I've been in London it's easy to see
There's no other Johnny looks smarter than me.
I'm going the pace, that means playing the game,
I'm one of the young dogs that's got a bad name.
I'm what folks would call a dare-devil, you know,
No sooner an argument, than it's a blow.
I've seen better days, and you know what it's through—

Playing the game in the West, playing the game in the city,
Leading the life that tells, flirting with Maude and Kitty.
Strolling along the Strand, knocking p'licemen about,
And I'm not going home till a quarter to ten, 'cause it's my
    night out.

To sing this, George wore a minuscule bowler, a jacket too tight, pants too baggy, large unlaced boots, a scarf that dangled between his legs, and gloves whose fingers were larger than his own. One of his comic effects, as he ambled about the stage, was the hacking cough that doubled him up in paroxysms of anguish—and his audience in paroxysms of mirth. He was in fact tubercular, and the cough was genuine and killed him after surviving World War I. According to her friends, Marie Lloyd never cared to stop and watch other artists who were on the same bill as herself, except for two: George Formby Senior and Dan Leno.

Before the present age of films and gramophone recordings, the only knowledge we have of actors of the distant past is what their contemporaries said of them, and also a kind of legend that survives in theatrical circles about their qualities. Future generations will have, thanks to recorded sound and films, a very fair idea—if only an approximate one—of what Sir Laurence Olivier, for example, was like upon the stage. Yet what is remarkable is that even in the cases of artists like Garrick, Kean, or Mrs Siddons, although we really know nothing about them from first hand, we do have a fairly clear conception of their style. Perhaps our impression is inaccurate, but in any case it is unquestionably *there*.

This must also be rather the case with Leno. There are a few pre-electrical recordings of his sketches which certainly tell us quite a lot. There was, so far as I know, no film, but there are numerous photographs, and drawings from the life. Most fortunately, there are also a large number of fairly detailed descriptions by writers, some intellectuals like Shaw and Beerbohm, others by intelligent fellow artists. (A few of these comments, like Shaw's, are hostile, but no less valuable for that.) Some of the texts of Dan Leno's patter have also been preserved as well as the words of his songs, which are mostly rather dreadful. There is further his autobiography, though this doesn't tell us much of what we really want to know. Yet all in all, there is enough evidence, I think, to make it plain that not only was Leno the sole artist of the Halls to whom the word 'genius' (which I think one should be most chary of using) could be applied, not only was he, without question, and together with Marie Lloyd, the most admired artist of his day, but he was even a chief figure in English theatrical history. No monument to him exists, he hasn't even got a pub, like Marie Lloyd, no street is named after him, no knighthood (as later on to Lauder and to Robey) was ever conferred: the only surviving shrine is his dressing-room at the Lane, which is still shown reverently to visitors. For though, as I have said earlier, he was much admired by Edward VII when Prince of Wales, he never became a 'public relations' figure as many Music Hall artists did when they sought, very naturally, to give status to a profession which, though admired by the multitudes, was considered, up till World War I anyway, to be inferior in its artistic aims, and certainly not reputable. For Leno was content to remain king in his own realm, which was the Old Mo, Drury Lane, and among his theatrical friends in Brixton. Nor, one feels, could he have done anything else: his temperament, as we shall see, was so unstable, his art, though so hilarious, involved him in such pain that he lived in a constant state near to nervous prostration. But for all that, every evidence points to his being a major artist; and as I try to establish this, I hope the reader will be indulgent to a greater degree of quotation and contemporary comment than I shall be using in the case of any other Music Hall star.

Dan Leno was born George Galvin in St Pancras in 1860 —'under the platform', he used to say, though the railway-station wasn't built then. Of this event he wrote later,

> I was born into the world a mere child, without a rag to my back or a penny to my pocket. Everybody—mark this —everybody has to be born, one way or another. You have to go through that inconvenience.

There was a sketch of Dan's called *My Wife's Relations*—in which the intermarriages became so involved that Dan, at one moment, cries, 'Well now then, follow me closely, will you? This is rather intricate': and such, one may feel, were the complexities of his own parentage.

For his father and mother, though called Galvin, were Music Hall artists who performed under the stage name of 'Mr and Mrs John Wilde'. There was then a second marriage of his mother to another artist, William Grant, whose theatrical name was Leno. Little George, when he in turn went on the stage, thus became for a while George Leno; but when the family was playing in Ireland, he altered his first name to Dan. This made many, afterwards, mistakenly think he was Irish, the more so as he stayed so long in Ireland in his boyhood as to pick up something of a brogue.

He made his début at the age of three[1] at the Cosmotheka, Bell street, Paddington, as 'Little George, the Infant Wonder,

---

[1] Not, however, equalling the achievement of his precursor, Joey Grimaldi, who made his at two.

Contortionist and Posturer', and wearing a pair of his mother's stockings, one red, one blue, hitched up round his neck with one of her garters. He was then teamed up with his uncle, four weeks his senior, Johnny Danvers, who was to be his partner later on in the pantos at Drury Lane. Of his early days in Halls as a child in Ireland (where he was noticed in Belfast by Charles Dickens), he was to say, 'I've earned a good deal of butter to my bread—but I wish it had been spread more evenly. Ah, I went through nightmare times when I was a lad!'

Over in the north of England, he teamed up with his brother Jack as 'The Two Little Lenos'. Here, in Manchester, he married Lydia Reynolds, and remembered 'four little people sneaking into a big church through a back door' and cold meat, potatoes and bread pudding for their wedding breakfast. But it was in the North that the breakthrough came. There was an immense vogue in those days for the now vanished art of clog dancing; and by studying expert practitioners, and even inventing new steps of his own, Dan won, in 1878, the World Champion's gold and silver belt against seventeen challengers after dancing every night for a week. He held the title till 1883, and when he came south again to London it was with the reputation of a clog dancer, and he used to display his championship belt on the Halls. Throughout his life, he remained inordinately proud of his skill at 'clog-walloping', and would on occasion still break into—to use the jargon—'twizzles and shuffles of the tip-tap-and-time'. It is recorded that he could silence an audience even as vast as that in the Lane by a stamp like a pistol shot.

His first date back in London (if we except his infant appearance at the Cosmotheka) was at the Middlesex, where he appeared as 'The Favourite Irish Vocalist and Acknowledged Champion Dancer' at £5 a week. He played as many as four Halls a night for years, devising new songs and sketches all the time, and building up a reputation. He has recorded that when passing Drury Lane, he knelt down on the steps at night and prayed for the chance to act inside. When Augustus Harris 'Druriolanus' spotted him at the Old

Surrey, in *Sindbad*, 'Druriolanus' offered him an audition at his own theatre. The impresario's method, on such occasions, was to sit by himself in the stalls of the huge auditorium, in the cold morning, summon the candidate on to the empty stage, and invite the wretched artist to make him laugh.

Harris told Leno he'd seen him in a Dame part, but asked could he play men as well? 'I *ought* to be able to, Sir Augustus,' said Dan. 'You see, I was born that way.' So he came to the Lane on a three-year contract, initially at £28 a week, and stayed on at the annual pantos for sixteen years at a salary that rose to £250. His first role was the Baroness in *Babes in the Wood*, but true to his promise to Harris, he played male parts as well. His chief colleagues were Herbert Campbell (1844–1904) whose beefy jocular bonhomie was a foil to Dan's excitable nervous energy, Harry Randall (1860–1932) and his uncle, Johnny Danvers,[1] who lived on as late as 1939. The girls or principal boys were chiefly Marie Lloyd and Vesta Tilley.

Leno's passion for performance grew to be so insatiable, that he appeared whenever he could, and even became part owner of the Grand theatre, Clapham. As his fame reached its peak, the absolute obsession with making increasingly demanding and ever vaster audiences laugh, possessed him: and not only on the stage, but off it, where it was always expected of him that he should set the company in a roar. He grew restless, increasingly nervous, never relaxed. Towards the turn of the century, there were breakdowns. Sometimes he forgot his lines. He became inflicted with imaginary grievances, bought jewellery and gave it away to strangers, and wandered alone about the London streets at night. Occasionally, he took rests and even spoke of leaving the stage so that 'I'll be able to retire on a small incompetency'. But he always came back, and grew to be haunted by the notion that he should play not pantomime kings and queens,

[1] Not to be confused with Billy Danvers, no relation, who also played at the Lane, and survived to appear with the 'Veterans of Variety' after World War II.

but Hamlet and Richard III. That they can play tragic roles is thought to be a habitual illusion of comedians, yet one may wonder if Dan mightn't, in fact, have got away with it. When he visited Herbert Tree at His Majesty's, he showed the eminent Shakespearian exactly how he would play the Crookback, and Tree was considerably impressed. 'If ever Dan Leno plays Richard III,' Tree said, 'it will be the greatest performance of the part we have seen.' And I think if he had lived into a later age, he would surely have been given his opportunity. For we have seen, in the cinema, George Robey playing Sancho Panza and more recently, Tommy Steele and Frankie Howerd at the Old Vic. All these variety artists played classic comic parts, it is true, but since Leno was, after all, a clown, and hence in some sort a tragedian, might he not have confirmed Tree's guess? At all events the opportunity was denied him, and he consoled himself by dressing up in the classic parts he longed to play, having himself photographed, and hanging these emblems of his frustrated hopes in his dressing-room at the Lane.

Towards the end, after an erratic performance, he got from an unsympathetic audience what seemed inconceivable for Leno, the dreaded bird. 'If I can't make them laugh,' he cried, 'I'll dance for them,' and broke into his earlier tip-tap-and-time. He died suddenly in 1904, aged forty-four, followed six months later to the grave by Herbert Campbell. Max Beerbohm wrote:

> So little and frail a lantern could not long harbour so big a flame. Dan Leno was more of a spirit than a man. It was inevitable that he, cast into a life so urgent as the life of a music hall artist, should die untimely.

Beerbohm's obituary essay on Leno is an unusual one in his theatrical writing. Max said himself, in so many words, that he didn't much care for the theatre, and although his reviews are brilliant and illuminating, they have rarely anything approaching a personal warmth or commitment. His attitude to actors is on the whole amused, often delighted, but rarely enthusiastic: they were, he makes us feel, extraordinary people, but not really splendid or, indeed, quite real. The tone of the Leno essay is quite different: for Max appears to have been genuinely affected and—what is rare for him—personally involved:

> He had, in a higher degree than any other actor that I have seen, the indefinable quality of being sympathetic. I defy anyone not to have loved Dan at first sight. The moment he capered on, with that air of wild determination, squirming in every limb with some deep grievance that must be outpoured, all hearts were his. That face puckered with cares, whether they were the cares of the small shopkeeper, or the landlady, or of the lodger; that face so tragic, with all the tragedy that is writ on the face of a baby monkey, yet ever liable to relax its mouth into a sudden wide grin and screw up its eye to vanishing point over some little triumph wrested from Fate, the tyrant; that poor little battered personage, so 'put upon', yet so plucky, with his squeaky voice and his wide sweeping gestures; bent but not broken; faint but pursuing; incarnate of the will to live in a world not at all worth living in—surely all hearts went always out to Dan Leno, with warm corners in them reserved to him for ever and ever.

One heart that did not go out to Dan, however, was that of George Bernard Shaw when he saw Leno and Campbell at Drury Lane in *Babes in the Wood*:

> I hope I never again have to endure anything more dismally futile than the efforts of Mr Leno and Mr Herbert Campbell to start a passable joke in the course of their stumblings and wanderings through barren acres of gag on Boxing Night. Their attempt at a travesty of *Hamlet* reached a pitch of abject resourcelessness which could not have been surpassed if they had been a couple of school children called on for a prize-day Shakespearian recitation without any previous warning . . .

A fellow performer, Seymour Hicks, may redress the balance:

> A small, frail person, shy and diffident unless he was among his particular friends, and with, to my mind, a tragic face, Dickensian to a degree and human beyond description. His eyes were like two wistful little black lamps, and his upturned nose with its big nostrils was well married to a large mouth turned down at the corners, which he always accentuated in his make-up, as he did the dimple in his chin. He had a strained expression both on and off the stage, and in his comic troubles he was as earnest as any man who suffered the tortures of the moody Dane ... He has a thin husky voice which reached every corner of the auditorium ...

The extraordinary face, indeed, is what everyone who saw him recalled about Dan Leno. There is a photograph of himself, Johnny Danvers and Herbert Campbell, with their heads one above the other, in which Campbell looks comically gruff, Danvers joyful and amused, and Leno ... what does his face instantly remind one of? Those deep lines down either cheek, the eyebrows screwed up in the forehead, that grimacing grin showing all his teeth, and those peering, vivacious, and yet somehow absent eyes? Immediately one thinks of the comic and tragic masks: which are really interchangeable, since the grin of comedy seems to be groaning, and the groan of tragedy to be grinning. So Leno was right, I think, in believing that a real clown was a tragedian ... which a comedian, however gifted, of course is not. For the clown, whom everybody mocks at first, is, in reality, however endearing, a lonely figure, alarming in his constant hint of disaster lurking behind the commonplace.

As for his voice, the surviving records—themselves, of course, distorted—confirm Seymour Hicks's description—and indeed, Leno himself said that when he became a comic singer, he had 'mislaid his voice'. As to his songs, their lyrics are inferior to the best in the Music Hall canon, for what he evidently depended on most was his patter, to which the songs were merely a culminating adjunct. Occasionally they have pleasant lines, as

> I like the Minueta
> But I liked the supper better . . .

and in a number like *I'll marry him*, in which Leno, as Sister Ann or some such character, is pursuing a swain lacking in ardour:

> My mind's made up,
> I'm going to marry him!
> He'll have to come to church,
> If he won't, I'll carry him.
> Five-and-twenty years I've had my eye on Jim,
> If he won't marry me, I'll marry him!

But it is really from the character sketches that we will have to try to reconstitute Leno's appeal—almost a forlorn task, since it is notorious that comedians' material, however gifted the artist, doesn't seem very amusing on the printed page.

We might first notice the remarkable life with which he endowed inanimate objects. Thus, of a cake,

> It looks as if it's got an extremely obstinate nature, but I think you'll enjoy that speck of jam in the middle.

Or the egg:

> Do you know, there's something awfully artful about an egg? There's a mystery in it. Of course, there are three kinds of eggs . . . There is the New Laid Egg (that, of course, is nearly extinct). Then there is the Fresh Egg, which is the same as the New Laid, but with an additional something about it that makes all the difference. But then there comes *the* Egg. That is the Egg I'm talking about. That

is the Egg that causes all the trouble. It's only a little round white thing, but you can't tell what it's thinking about. You daren't kick it or drop it. It has got no face. You can't get it to laugh. No, you simply look at it and say, 'Egg!'

One may perhaps feel that, for Leno, the Egg was a symbol of his audience.

His sketches covered a vast variety of London characters of both sexes in which Dan always figured as the resilient victim. In *The Moving Job* there is the hallowed theme of the brokers in, and 'shooting the moon'. In *The Shopwalker* he is tortured by a demanding (and invisible) female customer to whom he tries in vain to sell stay-laces, flannel petticoats and 'flimsy woolseys', and confides to the audience he's shopwalked such distances that 'I've only got the bottoms of my legs bent up to make feet. I was six inches taller when I came here first . . .' In *My Wife's Relations*, he becomes lost in the incestuous ramifications of his family, which he is conscientiously trying to explain in detail to the audience. Taking up the tale about half way through,

. . . And—er—during that time, our stepfather had married a third mother, and he'd pre-deceased also our second mother. So my brother met our third mother, fell in love with her and married her.

Well now, that's where the trouble commenced. Because, you see, that made me my brother's son, and my sister-in-law was really my mother. Well now then, follow me closely, will you? There was an aunt by marriage—she had an adopted daughter. Left to her for rent, or something. And —er—the—this daughter fell in love with the man that built the house where our second mother lives. You see where we're getting to? Well now then, keep close to me, will you? This is rather intricate. You see the uncle—oh! Oh, no, no, I'm wrong! I—no—yes—that's right! Oh, and—er —and there was a postman in it as well.

72

LONDON LIFE

The Grass Widower has a slightly sinister ring. Opening with an ecstatic 'And the wife's gone away for a week!' he explains how he saw her off:

> She turned round and said: 'You brute! You massive brute! I believe you wish I was dead!' (Isn't it *funny* how wives guess your thoughts!) I said: 'No, darling, but you must hurry up and get your train in the morning.'
>
> So I put the clock on four hours—we had to get up before we went to bed. But when I got to the station, I couldn't contain myself. I felt so overjoyed, I could have cuddled the engine. And I got hold of the guard, and I said: 'What time does it go?' He says: 'In five minutes.' I said: 'Make it off in two, and there's a pot of four-half for you!' He says: 'Shall I lock the lady in?' I said: 'Nail her in! Hammer her in!'

The sketch Edward VII liked most (and which earned Dan a gold pin as well as his title of 'The King's Jester') was *The Beefeater*. In this role, Dan prepares to show visitors round the Tower; but as will be seen, he really wants to lure them somewhere else:

> There's not a place on the face of the earth like the Tower of London. If you've never been there, go again. It's a glorious place, and supplies a long felt want. Everything old. And the first ancient item you meet is the man that takes your money at the door. Then you pass through the Refreshment Room, which is the oldest Refreshment Room in the Tower, and the only one. And there's some very ancient items in the Refreshment Room, such as the buns, and the ginger beer, and the barmaids and whatnot.
>
> Good-day, ladies! Do you want to see the Tower? Splendid day to see the Tower—nice and gloomy! Now—er —in the first place, this is the Refreshment Room. Er—of course, if you want anything in the Refreshment Room, now is the time. You don't care for anything? No? Thank you! Only as we go along, there's no oranges or ginger

beer to be hand, and of course, if you feel faint, you have to come back to the Refreshment Room. You ... No ... you don't care? No ... Don't want anything? No ... I do! Still—we'll proceed. Standing with our backs to the Refreshment Room, we get a lovely view of the Tower. Follow me, ladies. Standing with your backs to the Tower, you get a lovely view of ... er ... the Refreshment Room. Now you see that man there? That's the sentry. He stands there night and day with his gun fixed, bayonet fixed, and his eye's always on one spot ... and this is—er—the Refreshment Room.

I think our own age has produced comedians every bit as able as the best that appeared on the Halls, though I don't think their songs are so good—indeed, most of them don't sing at all, whereas all the older artists of both sexes did ... for it was, after all, the *Music* Hall they performed in. Yet I do not think that, since Leno, there has been an English comedian of equivalent poignancy: and one who, in having this quality, never fell into sentiment, but was, on the contrary, in his own madly poetic way, a realist. Nor can I think of any one whose range of social cameos was as extensive— and, for that matter, ambi-sexual. Nor of any who not only amused his audience so much, but touched them, for turning suddenly serious for a moment, he could sing with conviction *When the heart is young*. He was not a great tragic artist, if only because the whole Music Hall convention eschewed tragedy. But within these limitations he was certainly a marvellous clown, and the misfortunes of his own life seem to have echoed the part of sorrow that there was in all his comical interpretations. We may fitly leave to him a valediction:

Ah, what is man! Wherefore does he why? Whence did he whence? Whither is he withering?

Soldiers and Sailors

THE Music Hall age spanned three wars—the Crimean, the Boer War and World War I. Each produced scores of songs, and though the Halls were in general patriotic, one may notice a marked change of emphasis in each successive conflict. One element remains constant, which is the popular admiration for bravery and fortitude. But the haze of glamour and adulation that intoxicated the singers of the Crimean songs soon gives way to a marked element of satire in the Boer War numbers and, in those of World War I, to an undercurrent of lament. We may also notice how the popular pride in naval and military heroes is increasingly transferred from the splendid personages in the ward room or the officers' mess to the recalcitrant warriors of the barrack-room or below decks.

The patriotic tone of the earlier war songs is uninhibited and blatant. Their most memorable interpreter was The Great Macdermott (1845–1901, and really G H Farrell) who excited his already frenzied compatriots by the celebrated *We don't want to fight, but by jingo if we do!* which, together with other epics in this vein, earned him the title of 'The Statesman of the Halls'. (It was G W Hunt who is the forgotten creator— words and music—of this masterpiece.) I suppose there are not many today who would not blush if required to join in a hearty chorus of this number, and would not feel a certain embarrassment if invited to declare 'The Russians shall not take Constantinople!' (This referred, of course, not to the Crimean, but to the Russo–Turkish war of 1877.) And indeed, most of the Victorian war songs are fairly horrible even if only judged by the quality of their tunes and lyrics. All the same, I think we must master momentarily our dismay—and indeed nausea—at the tone of these ditties, and reflect not only that many modest souls of today might perhaps intone such numbers if we were as powerful now as we were then, and also that they do reveal, like distant and unharmonious trumpet calls, what vast numbers of our compatriots felt several generations ago about armies, navies, wars, and the empire they protected. In a more sympathetic mood, incidentally, the Statesman of the Halls, though he was also responsible for such numbers as *True Blues*, and *Stand to your Guns*, was the begetter of the still remembered *Dear Old Pals* (also by G W Hunt).

Charles Godfrey (1851–1900) was another enthusiastic flag-waver. Though in a more pacific and amiable mood he might greet his audiences with *How d'ye do, dear Boy?* (not to mention his lively *Hi–Tiddly–Hi–Ti!*), he was also responsible for such numbers as *On Guard, The Last Shot,* and *The Seventh Royal Fusiliers*—which last has indeed a rousing melody, still borrowed enthusiastically by such institutions as boys' colleges and Rugby clubs for their anthems, not to say war-cries. In those days—and indeed, even sometimes well into the next century—it was the custom of the singers to 'place' their numbers in cunningly conceived preliminary tableaux. Thus, in *On Guard*, Godfrey first appeared, dressed as a beggar, outside a casual ward. 'You're not wanted here!' cries the doorman of the workhouse with profound contempt, and orders poor Charles to be off. 'No!' cries Godfrey, drawing himself up into a fine military posture. 'No! I'm not wanted *here*—but at Balaclava— I was wanted *there*!' After this little bit, he must have had the audience in the hollow of his hand.

But the really symbolic figure of the British fighting man was the sailor, who is invariably depicted as a devil-may-care marine Don Juan—as, indeed, he often is. Ella Retford was to sing, later on, a number in his praise that is still known in every (surviving) vessel of H M Fleet, namely *All the nice girls love a sailor*—which is perhaps also true, except, maybe, in some cases, for the adjective 'nice'. Hetty King, too, who would appear dressed up as a mariner, and carrying this off exceedingly well—her business with pipe, kitbag (not that any sailor now has one), and deft expectation being beyond praise —gave Jolly Jack Tar's answer to all those 'nice girls' in her somewhat more realistic *Love 'em and leave 'em.* It is hard to realize now what with air power, let alone distant missiles, how ingrained was the notion, up till World War I, that the sea was the great protecting mother, and sailors the essential guardians of our shores and trade.

The heroic vision is enshrined in Arthur Reece's *Sons of the Sea*, whose lyric is so embarrassing that I forbear to quote it, though I have heard Reece in his old age thunder it out with such antique gusto that it carried a sort of melancholy conviction. *The Ship I Love* (words and music by Felix McGlennon) tells of a captain—merchant navy, this time—who refuses to abandon ship in a wreck, but gallantly commands his crew to row for the shore without him. This song was Tom Costello's, and it is a proof of his versatility that, in contrast with this heroic number, he was also, as may be remembered, the singer of *At Trinity Church I met my Doom.* 'You take to the boats, lads, praying to Heav'n above,' cries Tom, 'But I'll go down to the angry deep with the ship I love!' The cover of the sheet music shows Tom, equipped with a grey beard and an oilskin on the lurching deck of what is apparently a sailing ship, with one hand clutching the rail and the other tucked napoleonically into his breast while the yelling crew hasten to the davits. In fact, the whole thing appears rather improbable until one reflects that sailors *do* behave like this (even to 'praying to Heav'n above') and do so, even today, on countless occasions. Thus, once again, one is brought up against the fact that Music Hall sentiment is often fairly close to the truth.

A recurrent theme in naval and military numbers is that of the girl who's left behind by the boy who's gone away. *Goodbye Dolly, I must leave you,* sung by Leo Dryden (whom we will meet more fully in a moment) is a famous example, but a song of George Lashwood's (1863–1942) is even more to the point, because it tells us what the girl feels, not the boy. The girl in question has the brilliant inspiration of writing to her boy's admiral and asking him to look after her John—with disastrous consequences for the young matelot, of which George Lashwood, in later verses, makes the most. This girl's ludicrous—and touching—initiative is not so improbable as it might seem, since apparently, during World War II, captains of ships and colonels of regiments were inundated by letters from anxious Mums, if not fiancées, enjoining on them to do exactly what this young lady required. The song is called *Dear Mr Admiral*, the words and music (an exquisite melody) are by Fred W Leigh, and here are the first verse and chorus:

An admiral sat in his cabin
As the big ship sailed over the foam;
He was reading a letter delivered on board
As the squadron was sailing for home.
The grammar was rather eccentric,
And the spelling quite puzzled his head;
But at length he got hold of the meaning,
And these were the words he read:

'Dear Mr Admiral,
You'll excuse me writing to you;
But my young man is aboard your ship,
And I don't want him to give me the slip.
Will you please keep your eye on him as the time rolls on,
'Cos I don't want none of them Hottentot girls to pinch my
    John.'

But if the women were so sorry to see their lovers sail away, they did all they could to encourage them to do so beforehand. Lord Kitchener has the reputation of being the greatest recruiting sergeant England has ever known, but perhaps, in an earlier war, that title was already pre-empted by Vesta Tilley. She was born in 1864, and into the purple, for her father, Harry Ball, was Chairman at a Gloucester Music Hall. She made her début, like Leno, at the age of three as 'The Great Little Tilley', hit London at ten, and soon became a metropolitan favourite. Although a very pretty and indeed feminine person, she usually appeared in male dress, whether in a military or a civilian number. In the latter role she projected the original Burlington Bertie, and sang songs like *Algy, or the Piccadilly Johnnie with the little Glass Eye*. But it was by her military—or naval—numbers that she is best remembered, notably *I joined the Army yesterday (so the Army of today's all right)* with music by Kenneth Lyle and lyrics by Fred W Leigh, and the even more celebrated *Jolly good luck to the girl who loves a soldier*, by the same composer and lyric writer. 'Girls!' she cried, in the final line of the chorus, 'if you'd like to love a soldier, you can all love me!' Since she was appealing to the girls, but was dressed herself as a man, there is something slightly equivocal about this number—and indeed, Vesta Tilley is one of the few Music Hall greats (for there is no doubt at all she had an enormous and faithful following) whom I have not managed to find sympathetic, despite valiant efforts. It is not of course because she was a male impersonator— both Ella Shields and Hetty King were this, and each was entirely delightful—as also, by all accounts, was their renowned precursor in Music Hall transvestism, the ebullient Bessie Bonehill, who sang *The old tattered Flag* and died in 1938. It is rather that Vesta's voice, though it is admittedly most unfair to judge this by recordings, is shrill, peremptory and not very musical, and that while I can manage to find most of the 'heroic' naval and military songs acceptable, the militant patriotism—not to say, in the words of The Great Macdermott, jingoism—of Vesta Tilley's songs seems rather repellent. Of course, it must be allowed that many artists, usually non-military, had enthusiastic numbers in wartime, though not necessarily strident, as Marie Lloyd's *She has a sailor for a lover*, or *Now you've got the khaki on*. But the more habitual tone was that of Hayden Coffin's *The Soldiers of the Queen*, though this was sung at patriotic gatherings and not only on the Halls. And some of these songs do grate rather, the more so when a gifted artist like Vesta Tilley flogs the theme so relentlessly. In one of his World War I poems Siegfried Sassoon, on leave from the Front, writes of visiting a Music Hall and wishing a tank would come clattering down the aisle and blow the place to smithereens; and after hearing most of Vesta Tilley's numbers, it is not difficult to see what he means.

But even as Vesta Tilley was inspiring the 'girls' to inspire the boys to take the Queen's shilling, a note of disillusionment creeps into some of the Music Hall war songs. It is true the casualties were as yet comparatively light—at any rate, by later standards—and that the soldiers and sailors were still volunteers, not conscripts. But in spite of the ecstasies of Mafeking night, and the popularity of Lord Roberts and Generals Buller and Baden-Powell (all celebrated in Music Hall songs, though whoever sang the praises of the systematically unsuccessful Buller must have been himself something of a hero), the civilians began to realize that military valour was not being matched by military brains. And it was the cavalry man—the hero admired above all others in the days of the Crimea—who became, in the Boer War, the symbol of military muddle. Perhaps the invention of the motor car had something to do with it: popular wisdom may have realized, long before military tacticians, that the horse was on its way out, and with it, such flamboyant characters as George Bastow's *The Galloping Major* (written by Fred W Leigh with George himself). It begins to a rollicking—and, indeed, galloping— rhythm,

> When I was in the army I was a cavalry man, you know,
> And whenever I went on parade
> A magnificent picture I made
> With my galloping here, and my galloping there . .

and so forth. The infantry doesn't fare much better at George Bastow's hands. His *Captain Gingah* (both words and music by Fred W Leigh) is very much a barrack-room portrait of the monocled officer who is undoubtedly courageous, and undoubtedly a nit-wit: bursting with energy and incompetence. Yet it's a sympathetic portrait on the whole—satirical without being malicious, which was indeed, as I recall, pretty much the attitude of the other ranks to their officers—one of whom, in the army unit I first joined, was in fact called 'the galloping major' by his loyal troops as late as 1940. Here is the chorus of *Captain Gingah*:

Gingah! Gingah! they all know Captain Gingah!
Jolly old pot! O T 'ot!
Ninety-five in the shade, what, what!
I love the ladies! not one of them would I injah—
All the girls are fond of Gin—Gin-Gin-Gin-Gin-Ginjah!

But just as, in World War I, as we shall see, one of the most famous songs, and most popular in the forces, had nothing to do with soldiers, sailors or the war, so, in the Boer War, it was a civilian song of Leo Dryden's that somehow epitomized the period. Leo Dryden (in fact George Dryden Wheeler) was born in 1863, and became known as 'The Kipling of the Halls' largely because of his songs about the empire like *Great White Mother* and *India's Reply*. He did also sing military numbers, among them—still in his imperial vein—*The Gallant Gordon Highlanders* and *Bravo, Dublin Fusiliers*. But the song that lodged itself in most memories, and is still known today (though most public-house vocalists I have heard giving a rendition of it contrive to get the words more than usually wrong), is *The Miner's Dream of Home*. This is a real old heart-twister, tear-jerker number with an appalling lyric, though a pretty, if rather too fulsome, waltz tune. The Miner (who I imagine is in Canada) has left 'England's shore' 'ten weary years' ago, and his dream is about 'the old homestead and faces I love'. However, although one cannot exactly congratulate Leo on this number, one must feel sorry that, after World War I, the once universally popular Kipling of the Halls fell completely out of favour, and was reduced to singing about the Miner's dream in the streets until he died old and forgotten in 1939. As to why the song appealed so greatly during the Boer War, I can only surmise that it is so dripping with yearning for home that the troops and their girls both felt it expressed their own feeling.

Anyone who may still recall, as an adult, World War I, will also remember that the British army, in those days, used to sardonically call itself 'Fred Karno's Army'. Fred Karno (Fred Westcott, 1866–1941) is unusual among Music Hall greats both in that he is the only artist, so far as I know, who came from the west country—his home town was Exeter—and also because he became much better known by the artists he discovered than by his own performance. His Karno's Krazy Komics were the first of the crazy acts—later much imitated, both here and in the U S, where Karno troupes also performed—in which a team of inspired and carefully drilled lunatics worked together to spread chaos and confusion on the stage. He had also an indirect influence on the silent cinema, not only because Chaplin and Stan Laurel first visited America with one of his travelling shows, but also because his revival of mime led to the appeal of his shows being even more visual than aural. His two most successful 'gang' shows were *Jail Birds* and *Mumming Birds*, which were immensely popular just before and during World War I. Thereafter, as his vogue waned, he had the painful experience of seeing many of his own ideas return across the Atlantic in American film comedies, and after a belated attempt to break into Hollywood himself, and a vain effort to revive his fortunes by opening, in the 1920s, a pleasure garden on an island in the Thames he called Karsino (where the young Jack Hylton played), he retired to Exeter and opened a wine store. In Will Murray's *Casey's Court* there was a survival of the Karno style, and no doubt it had its influence also on the formation, in the 'thirties, of the *Crazy Gang*.

Among his artists who remained in England were Fred Kitchen (1872–1950) and Harry Wheldon, the date of whose birth I haven't been able to trace, and who died in 1930. Fred Kitchen's real claim to immortality may be his lecture on 'How to cook a sausage', which is rather like George Orwell's twelve (or however many it was) rules for making a pot of tea, in that both render an exceedingly simple process extraordinarily complicated. But his vogue among the military—

or at any rate, its other ranks—was due to his having devised a character called Private Potts whose resigned yet indomitable resistance to the hierarchy—even when this tries to court-martial him for breaking into a harem—won him warm approval as the embodiment of the eternal private soldier who has carried armies on his tireless reluctant back ever since men went to war. Harry Wheldon was another master of anti-heroics, appearing as a pugilist in retreat, and as 'Stiffy the Goalkeeper' who didn't stop any. Like so many comedians before and after him, he had a 'catch phrase' which in his case was "S no use'. And as a sailor in *So long, Sally* he rang a variation on the *Love 'em and leave 'em* theme in that, unlike Hetty King's ruthless mariner, who is quite heartless about the girl he abandons, Harry remains entirely devoted to Sally while making it equally clear he's overjoyed to be seeing the last of her when he bids good-bye to shore-leave romance and re-enters the tranquillity of the deep sea fleet.

With the arrival of World War I, the mood changes yet again for the tone of the songs was no longer so aggressively confident—their spirit is more one of an almost desperate determination to grin and bear it. For it didn't take everyone long to realize—after the first flush of 'business as usual' and the ardours of the 'first 100,000'—what they were really up against. What is more, when conscription was enacted, and the citizen became the soldier or sailor, he no longer thought of these, as in the two earlier wars, as somebody else who fought far, far away—but as himself: Private Potts, in fact, or Captain Gingah, who in 1914–18 was still very much around.

Thus, we notice that even Florrie Forde's *Pack up your troubles* is not exactly an enthusiastic number. In Charles Godfrey's song about the Fusiliers the key note is 'We carv'd our way to glory!'; but here is Florrie singing about 'troubles' and 'worrying' and repeatedly urging on the lads to smile— she uses the word no less than seven times in the chorus, and if anyone *does* feel like smiling, they don't quite need to be told so often. Likewise, George Robey's *If you were the only girl in the world* (which he sung with Violet Lorraine), one of the soldiers' favourites in the trenches, is filled with longing and regret: it's no more a case of *Jolly good luck to the girl who loves a soldier*, but of a 'Garden of Eden' to which both boy and girl are manifestly only too eager to depart, and there's 'nothing to mar our joy' as far away from the barbed wire as possible; and in their rendition, Robey and Violet Lorraine give it absolutely everything they've got of melancholy yearning. Perhaps this isn't, strictly speaking, a Music Hall song at all, since it was first sung in a revue, *The Bing Boys are here*, at the Coliseum. However, as Robey was a famous Music Hall figure, it can be embodied in the canon.

'The Prime Minister of Mirth' was born in 1869 and, like Chevalier, came from the middle classes and was, indeed, well educated. But the Halls beckoned, and soon he evolved his extraordinary, if somewhat irreverent, semi-clerical stage personality, in which he appeared as a sort of collarless unfrocked clergyman with a *décoleté* parson's long coat, a hat like a soup dish, and an attendant cane. His immense eyebrows rose in dismay when the audience laughed at his sallies, and he sternly commanded them to 'Desist from mirth'. He was a patter comedian rather than a vocalist, for though he did sing a number of songs, *If you were the only girl in the world* was his only memorable number.

It is said that in the sombrest hours of World War II, Winston Churchill fortified his spirits by playing, over and over again, Harry Lauder's *Keep right on till the end of the road*. Harry—or Sir Harry, for he was the first of the Music Hall knights—was indeed a stalwart figure in adversity, and in World War I his *The lads who fought and won* was a desperate rallying cry: desperate because when one hears it now—and the Lauder repertory is more fully recorded electrically than that of any other Music Hall singer—one is struck immediately by the melancholy of the tune, which belies the defiant affirmations of the words. Lauder was singing this song in a wartime revue when the news came to him that his only son had been killed in France. He went on that night and sang it, however, and since he recorded it after this dire event, the song catches some of the anguish which, despite his profound optimism, he must have felt. It is, in fact, a painful number, and sounds more like a dirge than the paean it was intended to be.

Harry Lauder is without any question one of the Music Hall greats. Yet I find myself a reluctant admirer of his art, despite his having been the most gifted of the singer-composers of the Halls, despite his having had the best voice of any and being an adept dancer, and despite his having left us, among dozens of successful songs, at least two Music Hall perennials— *Roamin' in the Gloamin'* amd *I love a lassie*. He was an ardent student of Burns and other Scottish poets, and there does undoubtedly survive, in his admittedly somewhat diluted and commercialized lyrics, some of the force and simplicity of the classical Scots ballads: so that if any Music Hall artist can claim to be, in something of the older sense, an authentic folk singer, Lauder's is the best title. He was also possessed of a fine baritone voice, whereas the vast majority of the Music Hall artists relied far more on timing, phrasing, 'character' and overall projection to deploy their numbers, than they did on their actual vocal qualities.

He was born in 1870 and lived on, in prosperous retirement, until 1950. The son of a miner, he worked himself in the pits, and soon took part in local 'smokers' and convivial concerts. He hit the Halls initially as a supposedly Irish singer—for the public was not yet attuned to the notion of a Scottish artist, and he had to camouflage, at first, his true style under the guise of such numbers as *Calligan, call again*. His first big success was at the Tivoli London—always a forcing-house of potential stars, and a pace-setter to rivals for discovering new talent—and by dogged determination, plus a sound instinct for publicity (for instance, telling the audience after his act that they must be sure to come again and tell their friends and all buy the most expensive seats), he overcame the Cockney resistance to the Scottish ethos with increasing, and then lasting, success. He toured all over the world, and became a sort of cultural and, indeed, national ambassador. In

America he was befriended by millionaires (including Andrew Carnegie, who advised him on investments), hobnobbed with presidents, and during World War I was an effective propagandist for American entry into the struggle. He was the first artist of any kind to sing to the troops in France—and to visit or sing to them not in rear areas, but as far as they would let him go up to the front line. For these services—even more than for his art—he was knighted. He later made a number of films, embraced recording and the infant radio as so many artists were reluctant to do, built himself 'Lauder Ha'' in Scotland, and became a sort of grand old man of variety right up until his death.

Then what can one find distasteful in this astonishing achievement? First of all, Lauder's aggressive, rather clamant Scottishness. 'Scotch!' yelled a Cockney gallery boy after one of his earlier performances. 'Aye!' cried Lauder, thumping on the stage with one of his celebrated (and later enormous) collection of funny, curly Scottish walking-sticks. 'Aye! Scottish and proud of it too!' etc, etc, and thereupon embarked on a sermon on the virtues of thrift, sagacity, grit, enterprise and so forth of the Scottish people (he said less about their bombast, insensitivity, and pig-headed arrogance). He did this sort of thing at the drop of a haggis, and such was the charm of his songs, and such the magic of his unquestionably forceful personality, that he won English audiences over and, one might say, fought the battle of Bannockburn single-handed all over again. He carried this rousing message to the world: he sang the praises of the stalwart Scot to enraptured audiences in Durban, Melbourne, Chicago and indeed every city where the loyal Scottish colony would turn out to applaud him in sufficient numbers, and persuade the doubting natives, to the advantage of Lauder's art and pocket, of the ancient glories of their race. He was, in fact, as well as a consummate artist, a shameless tub-thumper.

Then, there is the whole tone of uplift which, almost by his efforts alone, he succeeded—most fatally, I believe—in imparting to the glorious, ignoble spirit of the Halls. What was precisely attractive about them, in their most telling aspects, was that they were thoroughly unrespectable and cynical, and that they vigorously portrayed the worm's-eye view of life. Harry Lauder would have none of that. As has already been explained, the old Halls were giving way, at the turn of the century, to more sedate 'Palaces of Variety' intended for white-collar workers and their families, and Lauder climbed on this bandwagon enthusiastically. There was a strong tone of Presbyterian moralizing in his performance, and this went down all too well: he promised 'healthy innocent entertainment,' and added, 'I've succeeded admirably.' In his deft hands, the Halls became decorous, and this is one of the many reasons why they ceased to be the Halls.

It was not of course merely because he was Scottish that I am denigrating if not his art, his ethos. As we shall see, the songs of two other Scottish artists—Will Fyffe and Charles Coburn (whose real name was Charles McCallum)—were both well within the subversive Music Hall tradition. It is rather that he became a sort of public relations officer for an art that didn't need one or, once it had one so compelling, was already doomed. I must confess that, if I put on one of his records, and hear that resonant and indeed lyrical voice, and those words which contrive to carry into an industrialized era an older and entirely convincing rural magic, I feel like withdrawing these mean strictures. Nor was Lauder, it must be allowed, a merely vulgar puritan, as *Just a wee Deoch-an'-Doris* or *Stop your tickling, Jock* bear lively witness. But all the same, I do not think one can feel about Lauder as one must about Leno and Marie Lloyd: they remained, despite their resounding success, securely anchored in Hoxton and St Pancras, while Lauder was at the White House or ensconced in the serenity of Lauder Ha'.

One may notice as a postscript to the theme of *Soldiers and Sailors* that, if the songs about World War I were increasingly mournful and disillusioned, those about the ensuing war are practically non-existent. There were, it is true, in the early days of psychological encampment behind the Maginot line, such imbecilities as *Run, rabbit run* and *We're gonna hang out the washing on the Siegfried line*—something we did in fact manage to do four years later after colossal and permanent disasters. Apart from this, the favourite English soldiers' song, *Lilli Marlene*, was lifted from the enemy. Perhaps an echo of George Robey's *If you were the only girl in the world* might be said to linger on in Vera Lynn's *We'll meet again*; but on the whole, war songs were out,[1] and nobody regretted them, because the stridency of patriotic numbers now seemed totally inappropriate. All that survived, I am glad to say, were those soldiers' own songs which are never printed, but transmitted from generation to military generation in barrack-rooms and on route marches: all of them so candid as to prohibit their performance even in the earlier and more libertarian Music Halls.

Afterthought: Admirers of Charles Chaplin may have noticed that I have not hitherto included a detailed description of his art. This is not only because it is so well known, or because his Music Hall career was a short one, and his great reputation made in films in the US. The real reason is that I am not myself an admirer of Chaplin, or hardly so; and since almost everyone I know, and persons whose opinions I greatly respect, revere his art and use the word 'genius' about it, I had at first intended to disguise my own idiosyncratic disagreement by simply failing to describe his performance at all.

However, since I have spoken openly of all the Music Hall greats, it seemed to me, on reading the proof of this study, to be less than frank not to express an opinion about Chaplin too. To begin with, his name should certainly not be excluded from any portrait of the Halls, for even if his later fame was won on films, he was, both by birth and by achievement before he left for America, already an outstanding Music Hall personality. As for his subsequent career in the cinema, this is one

---

[1] The unfortunate French, in the days of the *drôle de guerre*, even organized an official competition among the troops for the creation of a rousing war song. The winner was called *La Gamelle à Gamelin*—a paean in praise of a general who was shortly to be ignominiously dismissed.

of the most extraordinary—if not *the* most extraordinary—in the history of the film, and indeed of the theatre. It is quite possible that at one time—and perhaps even today—his name, and certainly his face, were known to more people in the world—I mean the whole world, not just the Western part of it—than anybody else's at all; not excluding those of great political and religious leaders.

Clearly, it is not sufficient for anyone who wishes to question the claims made for Chaplin's talent to dismiss this phenomenon by attributing it merely to the immense impact of the cinema when, in its early days, it became the most formidable medium of mass entertainment that has ever been devised. This certainly accounts for a lot—as does the fact that, being a comedian who relied on visual effect, Chaplin's art was immediately comprehensible to millions of any language. No, clearly there must also be considerable gifts. What I want to question, however, is the greatness generally attributed to this talent.

In my opinion, Chaplin is a fine mime, an excellent comic, but not a great clown at all. As I have said earlier, to be this (like Grock, for instance), an artist's creation must be essentially subversive, basically tragic, and thoroughly disturbing of conventional complacency. Now, I know high claims have been made about Chaplin for being precisely these things: for being a sort of one-man social critic of the established order. But myself, I do not see his art this way a bit. To me, his 'little man' figure is pathetic, ingratiating, but not alarming. He seems to me to appeal for the audience's sympathy and not, like Keaton or for that matter W C Fields, to demand it as of right by confronting the audience with comic truths in a spirit of ultimate indifference to what the audience's reaction may be. To be entirely frank, I find the Chaplin 'little man' figure, despite the brilliance of so many of his comic effects, to be emotionally repellent. It does not engage my sympathies, chiefly because I am so aware that this figure is so insistently inviting them.

This I would say even of the early silent films, in which

Keaton seems to me to be altogether superior: far more astringent and poetic, and not, as seems the case with Chaplin, consciously pathetic. As for the later talking pictures, though I know these have been tremendously praised for their penetrating social and political comment, I have personally found their 'message' superficial and rather pretentious. Thus, considered as a satire on Hitler, *The Great Dictator* seems to me feeble in the extreme; or as a commentary on bourgeois sexual *mores, Monsieur Verdoux* not only unpleasant (in a sniggering sort of way), but entirely superficial. In films later than these, sentimentality and a rather rutty sexuality seem to have taken over altogether, while the earlier comic effect has almost vanished.

So if I were trying to assess who is the greatest figure the English Music Halls produced, I would unhesitatingly say Leno. This may seem absurd since I never saw him, yet I believe there was a depth and purity about his art which are absent in that of Chaplin. Chaplin certainly transported, with prodigious success, the traditional English comic art into the cinema, thereby influencing dozens of other comedians, and becoming the most formidable pop personality the world has ever known. Yet with the best will in the world, I find that celebrated figure with hat, cane and moustache chiefly embarrassing.

Work

As one might expect, the attitude of Music Hall singers to work is sceptical: at best it is deemed a regrettable necessity, at worst a tyrannical imposition. Since we are probably one of the laziest peoples in the world (though, if this stricture be true, Harry Lauder would doubtless have excluded the Scots from it), hymns in praise of the sanctity of labour are few and far between. In the primitive era of the Halls, it is true, there was a vogue for numbers of this nature, such as Harry Clifton (1832–72) sang in his *Work, boys, work and be contented,* and his equally rousing 'motto' song, *Paddle your own canoe.* The Great Vance (whom we shall meet in the next section) also weighed in with an admonitory *Act on the square, boys, act on the square.* But such clarion calls were not echoed by later singers, and Gus Elen's *Wait till the work comes round,* or Charles Coburn's even more parasitic *Should husbands work?* set the tone more aptly. Even Harry Lauder conceded that *It's nice to get up in the morning (but it's nicer to stay in bed).*

On the other hand, there are an enormous number of songs about individual jobs: in fact, I don't think there's one that hasn't got its song—certainly among jobs that are urban and, so to speak, retail; and even trades so unusual as pavement artist, balloonist, racecourse sharper, war correspondent, rat-catcher and night-watchman have their numbers. But we shall see that songs of life in mines and factories (on which England's wealth in fact depended) are much fewer, while rural existence hardly gets a mention, unless satirically, as in Harry Champion's *When the old dun cow caught fire.* Nor is there much that's realistic about what, in those days, were called the 'criminal classes'.

We have seen how Dan Leno, in his sketches, impersonated a great variety of professions. This was even more the case with his greatest rival as a clown, Little Tich, whose songs and patter evoked every trade familiar to his London audience. Little Tich was born Harry Relph, in 1868, near Sevenoaks, and he earned his nickname long before he went on the stage. It is sometimes thought he was called 'Tich' because he was small; he was indeed almost a dwarf, but in fact it is the other way round—he was the original 'Tich', and those so named (some men still are today) are called 'Tich' after him. The origin of his name was that he was unusually fat as a baby, and just at that time the Tichborne trial was in progress, and the claimant to the Tichborne fortune—a faker, as it turned out—was exceedingly stout. So the infant Harry was called 'Tichborne', then 'Tich', and when, belying the promise of his plump infancy, he turned out, as an adult, to be so small, he became 'Little Tich' and used this name on the Halls. (To make a tiny pedantic point, his name is often mis-spelt with an added t—'Titch'—but in view of its origin, this is incorrect.)

He made his début at the Rosherville Pleasure Gardens at Gravesend—the last surviving of those public places of general entertainment beside the Thames like the Vauxhall or the Cremorne at Chelsea which must have been delightful, and of which the present Battersea fun fair is a dismal revival. Perhaps the Tivoli gardens in Copenhagen are a better comparison—that is, until Miss Joan Littlewood succeeds in building a modern pleasure garden for us. (The neglect of the potential of the Thames-side as a place of delight is one of the dreariest failures of our city fathers, and ourselves: except in a few places, we turn our backs on this handsome river, which can now only be adequately, if fleetingly, seen from a steamer.)

Being so small, Little Tich hit on the happy notion of wearing elongated boots, several feet in extent. On these, he would suddenly rise up to a great height as if on stilts or, more alarmingly, lean across the orchestra pit at a gravity-defying angle, with his long boots preventing him from tumbling over. He was a favourite at Drury Lane pantos as well as on the

Halls, and greatly admired in France where he was given the *Légion d'Honneur* and the more fitting accolade, by Lucien Guitry, of 'the classic comedian'. But off-stage he was an unhappy man, perhaps because he was deformed (he had also an extra finger on each hand about which he was most sensitive, preferring to wear gloves), and perhaps because a taste for Little Tich was a rather specialized one—many seem to have found him repugnant, and alongside great successes, there were disastrous flops on some of his tours, notably in Australia—which country, if Sheffield be the comedian's grave-yard, might rightly be called his universal cemetery. He died in 1928, having outlived—like so many of the pre-war stars—his proper time.

I shall not quote from his countless sketches—builder's boy, grocer, waiter, zoo-keeper, gas inspector and so forth—because frankly, they are rather dreadful: seeming extremely unfunny, and slightly aggressive in tone. It is notorious that humour dates more than wit and, in any case, it is evident that much of the effect of Little Tich's act was visual. A flickering film of him does exist, which gives an idea of this. Yet even so, Little Tich remains, to me, something of an enigma. M Willson Disher, who saw them all, ranks him with Leno and Marie Lloyd as the three greatest of the greats, yet while I think there's not much difficulty in imagining why Dan and Marie were so wonderful, with Little Tich I find I cannot visualize his full quality.

Since I damned Lauder with faint praise, it is a pleasure to redress the balance by citing another Scottish performer who was, I believe, a finer artist than Sir Harry though not so formidable a personality. This is Will Fyffe, born in 1885 and, since he lived on till 1947, he belongs in time for much of his career to the post-Music Hall era though his style and songs were firmly rooted in it. We must perhaps excuse him for having launched *I belong to Glasgow* on a reluctant world (south of the border, anyway) since the singing of this, if such their caterwauling may be called, provides the Scots with yet another excuse to glorify their cherished state of patriotic intoxication. But his character studies of Scots of all ages and jobs were miraculous miniatures of observation, and unlike most Music Hall artists he was good at rural types—poacher, farmer, shepherd, village railway guard—as he was at urban figures like his justly celebrated *Ship's Engineer*, a Kiplingesque study of the Clydesider who really makes the propellers go round. He was wonderful at old men too—portrayed entirely without sentiment or forced 'character', and full of resigned and sardonic wisdom.

He was born in Dundee, where his father worked in the shipyards, and as a boy he lived with his grandfather who was a stock breeder, so that the two sources of his rural and maritime arts were familiar to him from an early age. Most surprisingly—in view of his later career—he first played Little Willie in *East Lynne*, and Little Eva in *Uncle Tom's Cabin*. He began to write sketches and submitted some to Lauder, who rejected them; so he studied them himself, abandoned the 'straight' theatre (where he had risen to playing Polonius), and descended—or rose—to the harder life of the Scottish Halls. But though he played Scots character parts there, he never blew the patriotic bagpipes as did Lauder: he was a Scot just as Elen was a Londoner—authentic and unashamed. When complaints were made to him that his 'Glasgow' song encouraged the Scot to go home drunk, he observed, 'He has to go home some time, hasn't he?' Luckily he made films in later life so that his art is not, like that of so many, entirely lost to us.

Vesta Victoria, abandoning her usual role of the perpetual victim of circumstances, also pops up as a working girl; but, being Vesta, of a rather peculiar kind—as an artist's model. The whole idea of artists—let alone models—is of course immensely comical in itself to any English public, and Vesta Victoria made the most of this, though her portrait is quite sympathetic if, inevitably, satirical. And being herself, misfortune does overtake her when she comes to the end of the chorus. This number is called *It's all right in the summertime*, and was written and composed by John A Glover-Kind.

WORK

My old man is a very clever chap—he's an artist in the Royal
    Academy.
He paints pictures from morning until night,
Paints them with his left hand, paints them with his right . . .
All his pictures—take a tip from me—are very very Eve and
    Adamy,
And I'm the model who poses for him in the garden all day
    long.

Oh, it's all right in the summertime,
In the summertime, it's lovely—
My old man sits painting hard,
While I'm posing in the old back yard.
But oh, oh in the winter time
It's another tale you know:
With very little clothes
And a little red nose,
And the stormy winds do blow.

This also seems to me quite a shrewd description of Royal
Academy painting, at any rate in its Edwardian heydey.

Copper-worship is a peculiar English trait . . . which many
mistakenly imagine is embodied in the familiar number *Ask a
P'liceman*. Incorrectly, however: for the English working class
has never shared with the bourgeoisie the love of the man in
blue. I recall, not long after World War II, that London
Transport brought out a series of posters in which the virtues
of various London professions were extolled in drawings by
Eric Kennington and ditties by A P Herbert. One of their
choices was, inevitably, the copper, and Kennington came up
with a sketch of a stalwart fuzz, and Herbert with a glowing
lyric. Across all of this, in an illiterate hand, some citizen (I
saw this in Camden Town) had written, in capitals, 'Old
Trouble'.

Ask a P'liceman, sung by James Fawn, music by A E
Durandeau and lyrics by E W Rogers, takes a cynical and
realistic line: what the copper will tell you, if you speak to

him right, is not what he should know at all. The first chorus
is deceptive:

> If you want to know the time, ask a P'liceman!
> The proper Greenwich time, ask a P'liceman!
> Ev'ry member of the Force
> Has a watch and chain, of course—
> If you want to know the time,
> Ask a P'liceman.

But in the second verse and chorus, James Fawn warms to his
true theme:

> And if you stay out late at night
> And pass through regions queer,
> Thanks to these noble guardians,
> Of foes you have no fear.
> If drink you want and pubs are shut,
> Go to the man in blue,
> Say you're thirsty, and good-natured, and
> He'll show you what to do.

> If you want to get a drink, ask a P'liceman!
> He'll manage it, I think, will a P'liceman!
> He'll produce the flowing pot
> If the pubs are shut or not,
> He could open all the lot—
> Ask a P'liceman.

In general on the Halls, where the copper isn't portrayed as
unscrupulous, he's considered comical: as in the series *Parker,
P C*, for which Charles Austin first got the idea when he saw
a police station marked 'To Let'.

Lawyers are regarded with scepticism too, though we don't
hear so much of them, since 'the professions' are rather outside the Music Hall range of interest—though dentists, if not
doctors, were painfully evoked in a sketch by George Mozart
(1863–1947). However, George Robey wrapped the legal

profession up, even if in a jocular and superficial way. Thus, from his sketch *Barrister,*

> All day long I'm standing at the bar,
> Swearing white is black, and black is white.
> If it wasn't for the fact
> Of the early closing Act,
> I'd be standing at the bar all night.

In the 1950's, in his old age a legendary figure, as Sir George Robey he reappeared briefly from retirement; and the audience, though sympathetic, seemed puzzled by the dated style. His son, Mr Edward Robey, is a distinguished magistrate in the London courts.

The criminal is almost a hero figure in French pop songs of the period—or, at any rate, a favourite one: Yvette Guilbert could send shivers down Parisian spines by evoking an execution in *Ma Tête*, and her songs of harlots and their doomed ponces were much admired. Of all this there is nothing in the English canon. Perhaps, as in the case of passion, this was due to reticence, or to a moral instinct; and so far as comic portrayals of criminals go, this silence may be because English popular feeling didn't find criminals, or their misfortunes, funny. If this be so, this reluctance is sympathetic, since jokes about people in prison, though much beloved by comic draughtsmen, have always struck me as tasteless and unamusing. Yet one does miss a serious popular portrayal of crime, such as was to be found earlier in W G Ross's *Sam Hall.*

The nearest we get to it is in the songs of Billy Bennett, best known for his *She was poor but she was honest* with its punch lines. 'It's the rich what gets the pleasure, It's the poor what gets the blame' (in the song, these lines come the other way round). Billy Bennett's personal slogan was 'Almost a Gentleman', and he wore a tail coat, boots, a waistcoat showing his shirt at the waist, for a fob a lady's garter, and he carried a flattened opera hat in his oversize-gloved hand. The number in question is *Don't send my boy to prison*, which is a narrative song, sung by the boy's mother, in which she relates his minor crime, and appeals in vain for human justice from the inexorable judge. Since Billy Bennett had a raucous, compelling voice, the number is effective, but it is scarcely pleasurable because the pathos is guyed, and the irony heavily over-stated.

Charles W Whittle (1874–1947) was a Yorkshireman, and appropriately, his finest number is about a Yorkshire working girl—or rather, the longing for her of her lover, exiled to the south and London. His most famous song, I suppose, is *Let's all go down the Strand* (Harry Castling and G W Murphy), but I have always found this a dreary ditty (like the street), with unmemorable words and a tune that's hard to sing convincingly. But in *The Girl with the Clogs and Shawl* the same team of joint composer and lyric writer have come up with a little gem—though it must be admitted that the lyric is not so remarkable as the tender, ecstatic waltz tune that it's sung to. (If the sales of this study justify the endeavour, I would like to persuade my publishers to print an edition with the music of the best songs as a supplement. Half the joy of a good Music Hall number is lost if one can't hear the tune and, even more, admire the dexterity with which the bards married the words up with the music.) Here, at any rate, are the first verse and chorus. As is often the case in Music Hall songs, the hero or heroine is the person described, not the person singing. We know already from Leno that clogs were still worn in the North, but to Whittle's London audience this must have seemed slightly exotic.

> Joe in London settled down,
> Left his little cotton town,
> Left behind his sweetheart fair
> Working in the Fact'ry there.
> And when from his rooms he'd spy
> Girls in stylish clothes go by,
> He'd say, as his window they'd pass,
> 'I'd rather have my little factory lass . . .

In her clogs and her shawl, little clogs, little shawl,
She looks fine,
And she's mine, all mine.
Other girls, other girls, may be fairy-like and tall,
But I'd rather be busy
With my little Lizzie,
The girl in the clogs and shawl.

The cases of Whittle and of George Formby Senior, may
remind us that, as the century advanced, provincial artists
were being made more welcome at the heartland of the Halls,
in London. There was evidently a lot of audience resistance to
overcome here, for it seems there have always been, in the
popular theatre, curious fashions as to which regions are
either 'funny' or, at any rate, full of 'character', and which
are not; and it required considerable perseverance by successful
artists to establish any such region in the popular fancy. Ten
years ago, for instance, Liverpool speech and people weren't
considered specially interesting let alone admirable, when lo
and behold there come the Beatles, Ken Dodd, and the whole
Merseyside vogue, so that Liverpudlians suddenly became
persons of fascination, even glamour. Thirty years before, in
the late 1920s, Gracie Fields had made Lancashire seem a
place infinitely desirable, and all its 'lasses' as admirable as
she.

Thus it was that artists from outside London had not only
to project themselves, but wherever it was they came from.
As one might expect, the earliest non-London characters to
be accepted as automatically of theatrical interest, were the
Irish. Part of the myth that arose from the English oppression
of Ireland was that 'Paddy' was a quaint, illogical, endearing
fellow, full of 'blarney' and inconsequence. (The other parts
of the myth were that he was a bloodthirsty assassin or,
alternatively, a barefooted beggar from the bogs, or else a
mystic with such head as he had lost in Popish mists or, yet
again, the world's finest fighter, dying to give his life for the
English queen.) Thus, from the early beginning of Music Hall,

Sam Collins was singing *Paddy's Wedding* and *Limerick Races.*
Before his death in 1865, W G Ross (although born in
Glasgow) had *Pat's Leather Breeches* among his earlier songs.
So strong did this tradition of theatrical Irishness become that
as we have seen, Lauder—that epitome of the Scot!—had
initially to present himself to English audiences as an Irish-
man. The Celtic stream soon became a flood, with such later
numbers as Lily Lassah's *Molly, my Irish Molly,* and Ella
Retford's *Irish, and proud of it too*—the tone now being less
comical, and more sentimental and aggressive. The whole
thing got quite out of hand in *Dancing 'neath the Irish moon*
sung by Dainty Daisy Dormer (1883–1947), though her real
triumph was in *I wouldn't leave my little wooden hut for you.*
There was even later the absurdity of an artist like Talbot
O'Farrell singing *Mother Machree* and *When Irish eyes are
smiling* to enraptured English audiences, despite his name not
being O'Farrell, and his English birthplace far from the
Emerald Isle. All the Londoners could do, in retaliation, was
to mock this spate of Irishry, as in Dan Leno's satirical *Mrs
Kelly* (he had a go at the Scots, too, in *McGockell's Men,* a
sketch about a gathering of unpronounceable clans). It is
curious to reflect (or is it?) that while Irish valour is praised
in Music Hall songs, between 1840 and 1920 there seems to be
no mention of what was going on there: the famine, the
tenants' wars and shootings, the Easter rising—all themes of
contemporary songs sung in Ireland, none of which filtered,
even in a diluted form, into the English Halls.

In the same way, once the Nigger Minstrels had established
their hold on tender London hearts, and artists from among
them like Eugene Stratton had gone over to the Halls, so firm
was the conviction that a Negro (even if really a blacked-
up white) was a romantic figure, that several London stars
had actually to launch themselves, at first, as 'coons'—among
them, of all people, Harry Champion and Little Tich. And
even when provincial artists portrayed themselves for what
they were, they had at first to ingratiate themselves with
Londoners by sending up their fellow provincials to some

extent. Thus, George Formby Senior had his comical Lancastrian 'John Willy', and even if Charles R Whittle sang *My girl's a Yorkshire girl,* he had as his signature song *Billy Muggins (commonly known as a juggins)* about a Yorkshire loon. Some provincials, like Tom Costello, who—incredible though it may seem for so fine an artist—came from Birmingham, kept quiet about their origin throughout their London careers. Provincial singers, too, were soon imitated by artists born far away, as when Florrie Forde from Melbourne gave her public *She's a lassie from Lancashire,* just as she had given them *Has anyone here seen Kelly?* in her seasons at the Isle of Man, a favourite resort of both Lancastrians and Irishmen. Apart from rural Englishmen, the only place singers didn't ever seem to come from—or to—was Wales: unless we include Will Evans (1875–1931), who really belongs to panto and the legitimate stage.

Another curious consequence of the rise to popularity of regional artists, is that the citizens of the region favoured by fashion started to imitate, and play up, this theatrical portrait of themselves. It is well known that, in France, everyone in Marseilles tried, at one time, to behave like Raimu, just as Scots were suddenly inclined to imagine they had become possessed of the forthright virtues extolled by Harry Lauder. Likewise, if Yorkshiremen (who are in fact exceedingly sentimental) suppose they are being 'plain' or 'blunt'—whereas they are in fact being rude and obtuse—this is largely because regional favourites have taught them this is what they are supposed to be. And today, when the North has become theatrically popular, broad accents full of 'character' pop up everywhere, sometimes in the mouths of those whose connection with these regions is really tenuous.

If Leo Dryden gave the Halls *The Miner's dream of home,* I have not been able to trace who perpetrated—for I fear that's the word—one of the few songs about what miners *did*: the celebrated—and frequently parodied—*Don't go down the mine, Dad (Dreams very often come true).* In the sense that this describes a pit disaster—or rather, the daughter's warning it is imminent after her dream—the theme is realistic enough, yet one cannot present the song itself as an example of Music Hall realism. The fact is that unless work was in some way picturesque, or pleasurable, or comical, we don't hear much about it on the Halls; and despite the invasion by artists from the industrial North, they told little of what went on there. Music Hall, on the whole, has an urban, consumer's point of view.

What is curious about *Don't go down the mine* is that some of the words of the verses, read without hearing the tune, are quite convincing:

> I dreamt that I saw the pit all afire,
> And men struggled hard for their lives;

But the tune makes it clear all this is a daydream—not even a nightmare—and when we come to the chorus, the words match the saccharine melody:

> Daddy, you know it would break my heart
> If anything happened to you . . .

We did use this song in the radio programmes I described earlier on, and I thought Clarence Wright just got away with it—for the tune is inappropriately pretty, and if you can bring yourself to sing the sentiment absolutely straight, the number is effective on that level. But the less said about this ditty the better, save as a reminder of the still-surviving divorce between industrial and residential England.[1]

It is a relief to turn from this to Gus Elen once again, who has numerous good 'job' numbers—in one of which, *The Golden Dustman*, the wealth fantasy crops up again . . . this time it isn't an inheritance, but the discovery, by the dustman, of

[1] As a matter of fact I'm not sure *Don't go down the mine* was really a Music Hall song at all, and am inclined to suspect it was a ballad published directly for parlour performance. But I include it because so many old-timers assured me they did hear it on the Halls—but if so, sung by whom and when? Help, please.

the loot hoarded by a miser who'd never let Gus and his mates empty the cans. When the miser dies, the dustman breaks in —no scruples about that—finds the treasure, and becomes *The Golden Dustman*. In another, *The Skipper in the Mercantile Marine*, Gus becomes that vanishing, yet once attractive and indispensable figure, the Thames bargee. I hope the reader will not yet be minding all the praises I lavish on Gus Elen, and would excuse myself for this infatuation by admitting he is my favourite Music Hall artist—in part, of course, because I was able to see him, but even more because his temperament, sturdy, laconic, tolerant and robust—so perfectly reflected in his harsh, friendly, sardonic, forthright voice—have exactly the qualities I most admire in Londoners, and miss most when I am not among them. He had also a sure taste in his choice of songs—even the greatest artists often come up with some dreadful numbers, but Elen never.

Here are the first verse and chorus:

I'm the skipper of a monkey barge wot 'orses 'as to drag,
But a penny steamer bloke's insulted me;
And the first time as I meets 'im I shall 'oist the pirate flag,
And a proper naval battle there will be.
Whilst I was on a distant voyage which took me quite a day—
'E goes and captivates my Sunday gal,
And she's sent a sneerin' letter, as she wants no more to say
To a person off a common low canal.

And she fancies 'e's the captain of a line o' battle ship,
But from London bridge to Chelsea is about 'is longest trip;
It's 'is uniform what's done it, but she must be precious green
To go and lose the skipper in the Mercantile Marine.

A chief comic figure among the tradesmen who call round at the house is, of course, the plumber. Not only is he traditionally incompetent, but he shares with the milkman (and the lodger) the reputation of a Lothario. The plumber's poet was Arthur Rigby (1865–1944), who delivered his chorus with bland innocence contradicted by a wealth of gesture:

I'm the plumber—I'm the plumber,
A very handy man in winter or in summer;
I can wipe a joint with ease,
But—well, touching ladies' knees,
It isn't in my line—I'm the plumber!

Equally light-hearted is the portrait of a new heroine of
the late Music Hall era, the nurse. In the days of Florence
Nightingale less was heard about her, for until quite recently,
hospitals were regarded as places you kept out of, even when
ill, if you possibly could (a sound popular instinct); and about
real sickness the Music Halls, in their characteristic way, are
silent. Thus, one cannot conceive any English audience admiring, as French ones did in Yvette Guilbert, a song of hers in
which she staggered about the stage as a consumptive, croak-
ing, 'Encore un poumon à cracher!'

So the English nurse, when she appears, is a charming
figure—as indeed, when off duty, she often is. This was a song
of Clarice Mayne's, who died in the year I write this (1966),
and who was married to Teddy Knox of the Crazy Gang. Her
tenderest number was *Joshu–ah!* (Joshu–ah! Sweeter than
lemon squash you are), and here she is on the fate of a patient
in the hands of a competent nurse:

Nursie, Nursie, nurs'd her little Percy
In a persevering way;
Nursie, Nursie, persevered with Percy
Till at last, so I've heard say,
Percy, Percy, married little Nursie—
It's a year since they were wed,
And now Nursie doesn't nurse her little Percy,
Percy nurses little Nurse instead!

This is almost a 'tongue-twister' number, of which the chief
inventor was Wilkie Bard, who died in 1944, and whose real
name was Billie Smith. Wilkie Bard cherished a deep admiration
for the Swan of Avon, so much so that he always wore a wig

with a bald crown and locks dangling over his ears. He also
hit on the device—which was bound to occur to someone in
the declining, or mannerist period of the Music Hall art—of
singing songs about singers, all of a ludicrous nature, such as
I can't hit that top note or, more desperately, *Let me sing!* As
he had, unusually for Music Hall artists, an adequate 'straight'
voice, his parodies are excellent, and it is perhaps fitting to
end this section on Work with a portrait of the Music Hall
singer himself: in this case a frustrated artist who, like Dan
Leno, aspired to higher things in other theatres.

The lyric is not inspiring, but the music is an effective
pastiche of a rather dreadful aria, as if by some Bermondsey
Bizet, and Wilkie gave it everything he'd got. *I want to sing
in opera* is the work of one of those hybrid teams of lyric
writers and composers, Worton David and George Arthurs.

> I want to sing in opera,
> I've got that kind of voice.
> I'd only sing in opera
> If I could have my choice.
> Signor Caruso
> Told me I ought to do so,
> That's why I want to sing in op'ra
> Sing in op-pop-pop-popera! Hurrah!

Holidays

IT is hard to recall that, apart from Sundays, most people in the Music Hall era had only three or four public holidays a year, so that these times off were especially prized and, by the singers, celebrated as rare days of bliss. And although everyone worked six days a week, Saturday evening was a time of rejoicing more fervent that it can be now when so many don't work on that day, or only in the morning. Indeed, Friday night has now largely replaced Saturday as the big night out of the week.

Sweet Saturday Night, which was sung by Victoria Monks (1884–1927) is quite a modest number, but with a pretty lilting tune, and words that exactly catch the feeling for the one night out, and the work that must so soon follow after it. And it is because this song expresses so perfectly the escape into daydream that the Halls provided after a grinding day, that I have chosen it as the theme song for this volume. (It has also, I think, in its craftily epigrammatic way, a title which, like those of so many Music Hall numbers, is apt and instantly memorable.)

> Sweet Saturday night,
> When your week's work is over,
> That's the evening you make a throng,
> Take your dear little girls along.
> Sweet Saturday night:
> But this hour is Monday morning—
> To work you must go
> Though longing, I know
> For next Saturday night.

There were also, of course, if not exactly holidays, the even-

106

ings after work when the boy met the girl on the street corner
or in the park. This event was celebrated by George Lashwood
(1863–1942) who was a versatile artist—he sang military and
patriotic numbers (as *The Last Bullet*) as well as comedy and
sentimental songs (including *After the Ball*, which he and Vesta
Tilley both used on the Halls, though it's really a ballad
number). Among Lashwood's best holiday idylls is *In the Twi-
twi-twilight*, whose tune—a lovely one—is by Herman E
Darewski Junior, with lyrics by Charles Wilmot. As will be
noticed, though this is a tender number, the authors can't
resist a mildly ironic dig at love . . . the passion which always
hovered on the verge of comedy. That the word 'spoon' for
love play has fallen out of use must be a great loss to lyric
writers since it rhymes with moon, June, tune and so forth.

> When a girl loves a boy
> There's no time they enjoy
> Like the twi-twi-light,
> And the hour of the day
> For which all of them pray
> Is the twi-twilight.
> There's a boy at the corner of every street,
> And his girl as she joins him is looking so sweet
> That he never once thinks of the size of her feet
> In the twi-twi-light . . .
>
> In the twi-twi-twilight,
> Out in the beautiful twilight
> They all go out for a walk, walk, walk,
> A quiet old spoon and a talk, talk, talk.
> That's the time they long for,
> Just before the night—
> And many a grand little wedding is planned
> In the twi-twi-light.

The obsession with food and drink emerges strongly in the
holiday numbers. There are so many songs about these that

one might imagine a race of gluttons, until one reflects that there was a lot of hunger, and a lot of poverty. What is noticeable about these numbers—as indeed about any that describe the good life (or the rich life) that was beyond anything but the dreams of most—is their remarkable lack of envy. If you can fill your belly, drink yourself silly, wear dazzling clothes and generally throw your money around, then, these songs seem to say, good luck to you. Indeed, from this point of view, if I am right in thinking the Music Hall songs do reveal genuine class preoccupations (and were not just daydreams cooked up by composers and lyric writers at the behest of capitalist impresarios), then they must be the despair of orthodox Marxist critics. The fact is, I think, that class feelings were not so strong in England as elsewhere, despite the existence of monstrous class injustices. If this is so, whether it reveals English working-class docility, or else tolerance, is a matter of opinion. At all events, if these songs are an indication, the English working class regarded the upper classes not as malevolent, but as profoundly comical; whereas I am inclined to think the feeling in reverse was that the working classes were both comical and reprehensible . . . that is the impression, at any rate, that volumes of *Punch* of the period now give when they portray the lower orders, and I think one may take *Punch* as revealing the popular middle-class ethos, just as the songs of the Halls did that of the workers.

Boiled beef and carrots, by Charles Collins and Fred Murray, is a splendid paean to pop eating. Although today the working class has much more money than its ancestors, when they did have any, I think they ate better: or at all events, in more congenial circumstances. Chains of restaurants offering pre-cooked and hotted up food, or even the regional caffs, are no substitute for the workers' cookshops that used to exist with their tall benches like church pews, and their heavily laden plates. These still survive here and there in London, and anyone who doesn't believe me should try one. The fish and chip shop, it is true, still flourishes, though perhaps not as succulently as when Kate Carney's boy offers, in *Liza Johnson*, to buy her 'a penn'orth of each'. I know it is blasphemy to suggest our ancestors had, in some ways, a better life than we do, but I believe some of them did, though not many of them, and certainly far fewer are miserable now than they were then. Indeed, what is astonishing about so many Music Hall songs is their entirely natural capacity to express, simply and convincingly, a state of happiness.

In this number, Harry Champion manages to mention, in one verse and chorus, no less than five delectable dishes, and I wonder what five one might choose today in an equivalent hymn to good pop eating. 'Derby-kel', by the way, is rhyming slang for belly, but I haven't been able to trace what part of the human body the 'kite' is. Any help here welcomed.

> When I was a nipper only six months old,
> My mother and my father too,
> They didn't know what to feed me on,
> They were both in a dreadful stew;
> They thought of tripe, they thought of steak,
> Or a little bit of old cod's roe,
> I said, 'Pop round to the old cook-shop,
> I know what'll make me grow:
>
> Boiled beef and carrots,
> Boiled beef and carrots:
> That's the stuff for your Derby-kel,
> Makes you fat and it keeps you well—
> Don't live like vegetarians
> On food they give to parrots,
> From morn till night blow out your kite
> On boiled beef and carrots.'

Harry also sang of the joys of smoking in *The End of Me Old Cigar* (Hurrah! hurrah! hurrah! They thought I was the Shah etc etc), though I don't think cigarettes—or even pipes—get a mention anywhere.

Songs about drink are innumerable, and one of them gave

his name to a legendary Music Hall artist, George Leybourne, or 'Champagne Charlie', who was born in 1842 and died in 1884. His real name was Joe Saunders, and he is one of the earliest provincial expatriates, since he came from the Midlands, and made his début in the East End. But sensing the popular interest in the 'chappies' and 'johnnies' of the West (the Piccadilly *boulevardiers* who have now entirely disappeared, and whose last survivor was possibly Bertie Wooster), he grew Dundreary whiskers, inserted a monocle, bought a squat topper and violently striped pants, and launched himself—thanks to the support of Charles Morton at the Canterbury—as the first and greatest of the *lions comiques*, as they were called: the upstart proletarians who, on the stage, were even more glorious than real 'johnnies', and whom, indeed, these very 'johnnies' from the West End grew to admire and even emulate. (More ponderous singers were known at this stage as *buffo vocalists*, while the female stage equivalent of the real life 'daughters of joy' were called *serio comics*.) Leybourne started in the Canterbury at £25 a week, and was soon getting £120—a colossal sum in those days. *Night is the time to have a spree, my boys* he told his audiences, and soon had everyone singing *Champagne Charlie is my name.*

Frankly, this isn't a very good number—neither words nor tune, as a film company discovered when they made a movie about Leybourne some years ago in which, though boosting *Champagne Charlie* as best they could, it didn't sound very effective. It must have been Leybourne's projection of it, plus his audacity in aspiring to be a 'chappie', that caught the public fancy so lastingly. In fact, it's not really till the 'eighties and 'nineties that the Music Hall composers and lyric writers really got into their strides, for when one comes to look up resounding numbers of the earlier decades, one so often finds them—deprived of the artist who first sang them —rather vapid and disappointing.

Leybourne's chief rival as a *lion comique* was Alfred Peck Stevens, otherwise The Great Vance, 1839–1888, who was a solicitor's clerk before he too bought a topper and cane and grew a formidable military moustache. *I'm the chickaleery bloke, with my one, two, three,* he sang to admiring audiences, and drove the point home with *I'm par excellence the idol of the day.* When Leybourne launched *Champagne Charlie,* Vance retaliated with *Cliquot, Cliquot, that's the stuff for me*—by J Rivière and Frank W Green, to whom, it must be said, the number doesn't do great credit. However, these 'drink' songs became immensely popular, and Leybourne and Vance worked their way all through the wine list until they came down to— if 'down' it be—the praise of *Glorious English Beer.*

But we must turn again to Elen for a worthy hymn to hops, and it is noticeable that, despite his singing to a tea-swilling nation, his contempt for non-alcoholic drinks is absolute. The number's called *'Arf a pint of ale.*

I hate those chaps wot talks about the things that they likes
  to drink,
Such as tea and coffee and cocoa and milk, why of such fings
  I never fink,
I'm plain in my 'abits and I'm plain in my food,
And wot I sez is this:
The man wot drinks such rubbish at 'is meals,
I allays gives 'im a miss.

Now for breakfast I never fink of 'aving tea,
I likes a 'arf a pint of ale,
For my dinner I likes a little bit o' meat,
And a 'arf a pint of ale;
For my tea I likes a little bit o' fish,
And a 'arf a pint of ale,
And for supper I likes a crust o' bread and cheese,
And a pint and an 'arf of ale!

In the successive choruses, the last line is varied to 'a gallon and an 'arf' and then 'a barrel and an 'arf'—bawled out defiantly, one may feel, at the Salvation Army lasses picketing the Music Hall doors outside.

  Clothing is another preoccupation. Today, working-class

boys and girls deck themselves out like peacocks, and are as sartorially splendid as those of any class. But in the Music Hall era, distinctions of dress were much more noticeable, and Orwell tells us that a well-dressed person, forty years ago, might be greeted by howls if he walked into a proletarian area—whereas now, of course, come Friday night, the boy on the building site knows he'll look far smarter than you do. Yet even so, it must not be thought that in the days of the Halls there wasn't proletarian finery—contemporary photographs prove this, as do many of the 'posh' proletarian characters the singers created—Kate Carney, for instance, for the girls, or Arthur Roberts (1852–1933) who was the *beau idéal* of every working-class male. There were, of course, those who had no good clothes at all and probably a majority who had few of them. But on *Sweet Saturday Night*, if they had them they certainly wore them.

But if smart clothes were admired, they were also mocked. J C Heffron had a legendary number about his hat—or 'tile' —and once again, even in this incongruous setting, the inheritance fantasy bobs up again. It was called *Where did you get that hat?*, words and music by James Rolmar, and between each verse and chorus, there was some telling recitative:

Now how I came to get this hat, 'tis very strange and funny,
Grandfather died and left to me his property and money;
And when the will it was read out, they told me straight and
     flat,
If I would have his money, I must always wear his hat.

(Spoken) And everywhere I go, everyone shouts after me . . .

'Where did you get that hat?
Where did you get that tile?
Isn't it a nobby one, and just the proper style?
I should like to wear one just the same as that!'
Where'er I go they shout, 'Hallo!
Where did you get that hat?'

112

HOLIDAYS

When Colonel South, the millionaire,
Gave his last garden party,
I was among the guests who had a welcome true and hearty;
The Prince of Wales was also there, and my heart jumped
    with glee
When I was told the Prince would like to have a word with me.

(Spoken) I was duly presented to His Royal Highness, who
    immediately exclaimed—

'Where did you get that hat?
Where did you get that tile? . . . etc etc.

And where did they go on their days off, if it wasn't to
Peckham Rye, the Welsh Harp, or Hackney Downs? The
answer comes chorusing in dozens of songs, of which Mark
Sheridan's *I do like to be beside the seaside* has the most
enthusiasm and bounce. It does need these, because it's one
of those 'rousing' numbers which, if the singer doesn't get a
firm grip on it from the start, is apt to flag. To sing it, Sheridan
wore his uniform of stove-pipe hat, frock coat, motoring
gloves, grotesquely bell-bottomed trousers, and battered brolly
which he thumped on the stage to reinforce his delivery. He
had several famous songs, the rather coy *Who were you with
last night?*, the celebration of another holiday event in *At the
football match last Saturday*, and his hit during World War I,
Here we are again!, which was a soldiers' favourite as well as
a civilians'. Like many comics he was a morose man off stage,
and after a hostile reception in Glasgow in 1917, he went into
a public park and shot himself.

    This misfortune may remind us that as well as going broke,
losing their popularity, and dying prematurely or forgotten
in poverty, many former stars also met violent ends. Harry
Fragson was shot by his father, who was jealous of his success.
T E Dunville (1868–1924) drowned himself in the Thames at
Reading. One often hears Music Hall comics described disdainfully (by those who never saw them) as 'red-nosed comedians',
but none of the great stars, in their make-up, did anything so

E   113

obvious and humourless. T E Dunville, though, is an exception —he did accentuate the grotesque in his stage appearance (circus clown make-up, clothes either too baggy or too small), though apparently he carried this off with a Keaton-like equanimity. To read, his songs and material seem remarkably unfunny—he specialized in 'ruthless rhymes', and had numbers with titles like *Bunk—A—Doodle—I—Do* and *Pop, Pop, Popperty—Pop* for which it is hard now to feel even an historical enthusiasm. However, he was an admired star in the 'nineties and the Edwardian era, and when fashions swiftly changed, and they no longer laughed, it was too much for him. Although I said earlier that Music Hall artists, however tragic their own lives might sometimes be, eschewed tragedy on the Halls, we should notice that there were two 'suicide' songs of Charles Godfrey's (he of *The Seventh Royal Fusiliers*)—*The Lost Daughter* and *Across the Bridge*; but I have not been able to discover if these were taken 'straight' or sentimentally—I would guess the latter.

Another song, *Brighton*, celebrates London-on-the-sea, which is also the setting for Harry Fragson's tactless enquiries in *Hullo! Hullo! Who's your lady friend?* *Brighton* was sung by R G Knowles, billed as 'The Very Peculiar American Comedian', who was in fact born in Ontario, in 1858, and lived on till 1919. Unlike two of the other North Americans who became stars in England, Eugene Stratton and Ella Shields, Knowles never 'blacked up', but presented himself to the English public dressed like a US Senator of the period though with a rather surprising crew cut. He had run away from home to Chicago, and worked among miners in Colorado, where he made his début in a country saloon at $25 a week plus coins thrown at him by the gamblers. When he appeared at the Olympic, Chicago, he boldly told his audience if they didn't laugh they weren't getting their money's worth, whereupon the manager hauled him off stage, amid loud applause. He moved to the National in New York, joined Haverley's Minstrels for a while, worked with Daly's company in the legitimate theatre, but after a quarrel, opened in London at the Trocadero in 1891 amid 'an outburst of enthusiastic silence' as he relates it. But the silence soon vanished for he had the happy knack, rare in its day, of not only delivering his prepared patter, but engaging in spontaneous badinage with the audience, often of an argumentative nature, so that his act often ended in a real, rather than a simulated, row. But this seemed to go down well with the gallery boys and their donahs, and he played long seasons at the Empire and the Tivoli. One of his early English friends was Charles Chaplin Senior who was a star in his own right, and whose son was to cross the Atlantic in the reverse direction to R G Knowles's. Yet another expatriate who may be recorded here is George Leyton, 1864–1948, who was from New Orleans, but who became so thoroughly acclimatized (*Boys of the Chelsea School*, and so on) that not much American was left of him.

But the praises of a good blow on the front at all those seaside resorts which came to festoon the English coast towards the end of the last century, was not a universal one. Dan Leno had a song called *Never More* about the horrors of marine life, and Wilkie Bard's famous tongue-twister, *She sells sea-shells*, declares that 'the sea-shells she sells are a terrible sell'. Some brave spirits ventured across the channel, and according to George Lashwood, this often had sickening results. In his *Sea, sea, sea*, the chorus, to a hideously deft tune, begins to lurch horribly:

> Sea, sea, sea,
> Oh, why are you so angry with me?
> Ever since we left Dover
> I thought the boat would go over . . .

and so on.

Despite these tribulations, Cockneys sometimes did succeed not only in getting to France, but staying there a while— though only, presumably, if they were well off, since 'Gay Paree' was more of a legend than a reality for most. (France seems to have been the only Continental target, though Mary Moore Duprez did get *By the side of the Zuider Zee*.) Marie

Lloyd Junior relates that her mother, after her second marriage to Alec Hurley, visited the French capital, but was depressed by it. So much so that when Hurley took her for a drive up the Champs Elysées to cheer her up, only to find his new bride growing gloomier, he cried to the coachman, '*Cocher— retournez!* Madam's got the bloody 'ump.' Perhaps it was as a consequence of this excursion that Marie bought the song *The Coster Girl in Paris.* I haven't been able to trace the authors of this, but though it's not one of Marie's great numbers, it's a characteristic one in a sense since it reveals the almost fanatical local patriotism of the Londoner. It may seem absurd to prefer the 'Ackney Road to the Champs Elysées, but evidently Marie did, and so no doubt would most of her audience. Paris, to them, was just, in Marie's words, 'a proper pantomime'. Of the four songs Marie recorded (all pre-electrical, alas), this one survives the best . . . the old disc doesn't give much volume, but the vivacity and the friendly, assured impertinence of her voice, come over loud and clear.

Seen the twinkle in me eye?
Just come back from France, that's why—
Me and Bill went over there to spend our 'oneymoon.
First time I'd been in foreign parts,
Did I like it? Bless your hearts!
Can't say any more than that it ended up too soon.
But don't think I've done with good old England—not likely,
Born and bred down 'Ackney road, ah! an' proud to own it too.
You like me make up?
Ain't it great?
The latest thing from Paris—straight!
Gives a girl a chance to show you what she can do!

And I'd like to go again
To Paris on the Seine,
For Paris is a proper pantomime,
And if they'd only shift the 'Ackney road and plant it over
    there,
I'd like to live in Paris all the time.

The most celebrated Music Hall traveller to 'foreign parts' was without doubt Charles Coburn (1852–1945) who launched on the world *The Man who broke the bank at Monte Carlo.* Coburn was a Scot, born Charles Whitton McCallum, and before the success of Lauder in establishing the Scot as a Music Hall character, Coburn tried in vain to captivate London audiences with Scottish sketches as Charles Laurie. Not only the act but the name seemed wrong, so passing down Coburn Street, E 1, one day, he asked himself, why not that? His first real success came with *Two lovely black eyes.* The tune of this, by Edmund Forman, really belongs to *My Nelly's Blue Eyes* which the Christy Minstrels had made popular, and Coburn thought it might go over in a parody. So he offered his own version at the Trocadero, where it got off to a sticky start, being at first only applauded by loyal and indulgent members of the Moore and Burgess Minstrels who came on from the St James's Hall nearby to support Coburn in his plagiarism. But thanks, no doubt, to the punch line 'Oh what a surprise!' it soon caught on—helped, perhaps, by political passions, for it is not usually known that the reason for Coburn's getting the black eyes was that he 'praised the Conservatives frank and free', whereas his adversary was a Liberal.

It was Fred Gilbert who wrote the words and music of *The Man who broke the bank at Monte Carlo,* and the idea came to him on seeing a poster in the Strand announcing this lucky happening. He offered it to Chevalier, who turned it down, and so at first did Coburn, thinking—in his own words—that it was 'rather too highbrow for the average Music Hall audience'. One can easily see what he meant, for the words are quite intricate and the time of the tune *presto,* but Coburn got over this by relentlessly plugging the number to initially reluctant audiences. When he launched it at the Oxford, he sang the chorus after the last verse no less than ten times, whether the audience liked it or not, and Coburn became, as the number gathered strength, what one might call the pioneer of song-plugging. It is rather hard to realize now, when a

number can be projected so quickly and emphatically by so
many mechanical means, what a struggle a Music Hall artist
had to rescue a favourite song from the oblivion that awaited
so many of the thousands of numbers that were optimistically
launched upon the Halls. There was only sheet music to help,
but until enough people had heard the number in the flesh,
there wouldn't be any buyers unless the artist was already
well known. I don't myself think that *T M W B T B A M C*
is, despite its success, a really notable song, but anyone interested in judging of this can still hear it, for thanks to his living
to a great age, Coburn was able to put all his best numbers on
to electrical recordings.

For most Londoners, however, Monte Carlo might have
been in Japan, and even the seaside was too far away: for as
Billy Williams plaintively put it, *Why can't we have the sea in
London?* Billy Williams (1877–1915) was, like Florrie Forde
and Albert Whelan, an Aussie, who started life in a Melbourne
racing stable, then became a boundary rider on an outback
station. In 1895, he joined one of the variety companies that
used to tour the back blocks and play to highly critical bush
audiences. (I remember a survivor of these bush touring
troupes as late as the 1920s, whose comedian, dressed as a
woman, sent the rural Aussies into fits by pretending to be in
love with the local storekeeper, who was sitting in the audience
of at most forty, many of whom had ridden in for miles to see
the show). Trained in this hard school, Billy came to London
in 1900 to the Marylebone, and soon became known as an
urbane and cordial performer who didn't wear funny clothes,
but only the dress that won him the title of 'The Man in the
Velvet Suit'. Perhaps because he was an Australian, and wasn't
afraid of novelty, he early embraced gramophone recording,
and some twenty songs of his survive—pre-electrical, but
luckily quite audible. Williams was specially liked for his gaiety
and unforced laughter, and what is really remarkable is that
this quality comes over even on his records—in which he
appears to be enjoying himself immensely. His most popular
number is *When father papered the parlour*, by Weston and

Barnes, and I include it here because though papering was
not exactly a holiday undertaking, Billy Williams makes it
sound like one; and anyway, lots of citizens use holidays for
catching up on household chores. Chorus:

When father paper'd the parlour you couldn't see Pa for paste!
Dabbing it here, dabbing it there—
Paste and paper ev'rywhere.
Mother was stuck to the ceiling,
The children stuck to the floor:
I never saw a blooming family so stuck up before.

Not in cold print a very inspired lyric, but Billy Williams
makes it irresistible.

Holidays are associated with going somewhere else, and
songs about means of transport are numerous . . . though
curiously, even if we have horses, donkeys, hansom cabs, cars,
bicycles, omnibuses, trams, metropolitan tubes, and even
balloons, I don't know any number about a train—unless we
count Will Fyffe's *The Stationmaster*, in which the rural train
has difficulty in catching up with a cow. I can't think of any
reason for this, unless it might be that trains recalled too
much the industrial England that the Music Halls seemed
determined to ignore. *Daisy Bell*, music and words by Harry
Dacre, is of course the famous bicycle song, though I confess
it's not one of my favourites since it seems to belong to musical
comedy more than to Music Hall. I prefer Fred Coyne's earlier
The Velocipede about a three-wheeler propelled from the front,
with which he created a sensation by riding it on to the stage
amid 'bursts of applause', according to the song-sheet cover.
Katie Lawrence, who sang *Daisy Bell*, made such a success out
of it in England and the US—it even became one of the rare
Music Hall numbers well known in Continental Europe—
that she was able to build Bell House near the zoo until, after
her husband's death, she fell on evil days and though helped
by Marie Lloyd, died in poverty in 1915.

Motor cars were a gift to the Music Hall bards, who instantly spotted their comic possibilities, as in Gerald Kirby's *He'd have to get under (get out and get under)* which makes the inevitable point,

A dozen times of love he'd try to speak,
And then the radiator it would leak . . .

But the most famous epic of automobile disaster was Harry Tate's *Motoring*—much beloved of Edward VII and even of his consort, so that Tate billed himself as 'The Man who made the Queen laugh'.

He was born Ronald Macdonald Hutchinson in Scotland, in 1872, where he worked as a lad for Henry Tate and Sons, the sugar refiners, whose name he adopted when he broke into the Halls.[1] His début was at the Oxford in 1895, and in association with Wal Pink he devised a series of sketches that were a comic commentary on contemporary *mores*: *Fishing, Golfing, Selling a Car* and *Motoring* in particular. (If you relied on this kind of sketch rather than on songs, you were known as a 'descriptive vocalist'.) Harry's company consisted of a group of appalling and lugubrious boys, exceedingly civil yet totally unhelpful in Harry Tate's predicaments—among them, for no reasons at all, a person called 'Kennedy' and Harry's 'son' who exasperated him by making helpful suggestions to 'Pa-Pa' in a strained falsetto when everything went wrong. Like W C Fields, to whom all inanimate objects were deadly enemies, Harry Tate, for all his earnest solemnity about the job in hand, could never get anything to function as it was meant to. Restraining himself, however, with saintly patience, he would only exhibit his exasperation by causing his moustache to twirl round in a circle like a propeller blade. When the Halls declined, he managed—as so many failed to—to make the switch, and was successful in revue and silent films. He lived on till 1940, and was thus able to record some

[1] I have given some of the curious and varied reasons for which artists chose stage names . . . my own favourite choice is Bud Flanagan's, who named himself after a particularly loathsome Sergeant-major in World War I so as to make sure the CSM would be laughed at in perpetuity.

of his best sketches which, considering that the visual element is entirely lacking, and that cars and golfing are no longer novelties, stand up very well. 'Kennedy' and his 'son' take part on these recorded performances, and after hearing one of Tate's disks you feel almost as inclined to wring their necks as he did; yet despite all provocation by man and machine, Harry maintains throughout a noble if desperate composure.

I recall that on an infant visit to the country, some time during World War I, a displaced London nanny (not my own, for she came from Lincolnshire) warned me with marked distaste against 'those nasty cows'; and one may search the Music Hall songs in vain for accounts of delightful excursions to anywhere outside the cities except the sea. Wilkie Bard, it is true, in *Truly Rural*, tells of the country but only to mock it, and Gus Elen, though his Cockney characters like urban foliage, expresses in one of his songs the opinion that *Nature's made a big mistake*. Perhaps one may discern a faint sympathy for the country in Ellaine Terriss's *Honeysuckle and the bee*, though insect and plant are really a metaphor for human 'spooning'. As for Gertie Gitana's celebrated *Nelly Dean*, and its rhapsodies about 'an old mill by the stream' and 'the waters where they flow', this is a city fantasy, for the number has no sense of time or place—it is indeed the very fact it is so abstract and unreal that, coupled with its gooey tune, makes it such a public-bar favourite. We may also notice that if Londoners didn't want to go to the country, they considered it equally imprudent for a country girl to come to London. Alice Leamar has a distressing number called *Her golden hair was hanging down her back* about a rural lass who ventures into the big city where what might be expected happens, so that

> Alas and alack! She came back
> With a naughty little twinkle in her eye . . .

for the collapse of her hair is the symbol of a more serious fall.

And if Londoners did gird up their loins and wrench themselves away from the city on a rural excursion, it wasn't for long. George Lashwood has a song called *Riding on top of the car* in which he takes his girl on a tramcar to the country, in search—so he avers—of 'a quiet country lane' and 'an old rustic stile' . . . but what does he do when the tram reaches the terminus?

> We get to the end of the journey all right,
> Or, at least, to the end of the track,
> But while all the others prepare to alight,
> We remain on the car and go back.

Of course, George was with his girl, and as he tells us later, trams are 'cosy' and 'the seats are so small', but all the same . . . no, it must be admitted Cockneys don't *like* the country (not that they knew anything about it), and it will be recalled how, in World War II, evacuated city children were so appalled by rural peace and safety, that they beseeched their fond Mums to let them return to the happy life of the bomb shelter. I also remember, when inducted into the extremely rural Wiltshire regiment at that time, the profound contempt of the London boys for the local 'swede-bashers': one reciprocated, of course, but the Cockneys didn't deign to notice this. Perhaps one reason why the country doesn't seem an appealing place is that in the Music Hall era, no great singers from the rural counties appeared to praise it: Londoners, Lancastrians, Yorkshiremen, Scots and Irish are the chief artists, though Lauder, certainly, sang of his 'highland lassie'—but that was far off in improbable Scotland, and not in some dreadful place like Cumberland, or Devonshire, or even Essex.

I think it is something of a triumph to write a romantic number about a tram—for having been raised in the tram-ridden city of Melbourne, I have a horror of this vehicle; but this is evidently not shared by many townsmen, for when the last London tram made its farewell journey after World War II, dozens of enthusiasts travelled over Westminster bridge in it with tears pouring down their cheeks. *Riding on top of the car* has music by Harry von Tilzer and lyrics by Fred W

HOLIDAYS

Leigh and V P Bryan, and it's a lovely waltz tune that's just right for George Lashwood's tone of ecstasy.

> Some people declare that a quiet country lane
> Is the very best place for a spoon;
> An old rustic stile must be there, they'll explain,
> And not too much light from the moon.
> Now, my girl and I live in town, you must know,
> Where quiet country lanes can't be found;
> We've got no rustic stile in our neighbourhood, so
> Ev'ry time Sunday ev'ning comes round . . .
>
> Then we go, go, go for a ride on a car, car, car,
> For you know how cosy the tops of the tramcars are—
> The seats are so small, and there's not much to pay,
> You sit close together and spoon all the way,
> There's many a Miss will be Mrs some day
> Through riding on top of the car.

So back they all come to London: where the last word, as so often, belongs to Gus Elen, who has a song about taking out his wife and numerous children, on a bank holiday, all round the sights of the capital, covering most of the Greater London area before nightfall amid mounting disasters, and with a final line to each resolutely despairing chorus of, *I'm glad we had a nice quiet day.*

123

Friendship

THE Music Hall canon sets great store by friendship. This, it turns out, can be of several kinds. First of all, the friendship among men—often after a quarrel, and despite this. Indeed, there are more invocations of friendship after a row has happened, than among friends who've never much quarrelled at all.

With young lovers, friendship can't exist, because that's not what they want: they want marriage, or at any rate the girl does. But if the lovers quarrel and 'part', friendship is still possible—or, at all events, the girl often claims it is, though we may not quite believe her, and may notice that the boy has much less to say on this reassuring theme.

Then there is the friendship of the ageing married couple. Love, in the Music Hall world, is, as I have said, a blissful dream for the courting boy and girl, with roses, roses all the way. But after the wedding bells have tolled their festive knell, love flies out of the window and married life becomes a comic misfortune. But if the old boy and girl have lived long enough together, the nagging and bickering pass away, and they achieve a certain dignity and agreement. There are many songs about the old couple who, all passion spent, are united by the deeper—if much less interesting—bond of friendship.

There are dozens of numbers describing all these situations, yet not one, so far as I can discover, that essentially rejects the marriage bond. Infidelity of course exists, or at any rate is implied (all those marauding milkmen and plumbers, and all those *Girls, Girls, Girls!* as Charles R Whittle cried in a moment of wild abandon), but from such adventures you return inexorably to the wry imperatives of the marriage bed. I think one may assume that, in the period we're discussing, this *was* more or less what happened: for so many songs say

124

this, and with such conviction, that if it were not so, the audiences would surely have laughed their heads off. This is not to deny the Music Hall picture of relations between men and women is an idealized one, yet evidently the audiences accepted this ideal, even if they did not always conform to it themselves. Hypocrisy? Sentimentality? Or was it just what they did feel and wanted to do?

Comrades, sung by Tom Costello, to words and music by Felix McGlennon, is a good example of the first instinct I have mentioned. It's sentimental, of course ('Sharing each others' troubles, Sharing each others' joys . . .'), but here again we come up against the difficulty for those who reject sentiment on all occasions, that however corny some human situations may be, they do exist as such. If anyone is understandably doubtful whether such a song can be convincing, they could listen to Tom Costello singing this: for artistically, he makes his point. It's also nice, by the way, when the word 'comrade' has been so debased by political philosophers into a term of bullying blackmail, to hear its real meaning restored to it again.

Bessie Bonehill, though a buxom woman, was a male impersonator, so that she was able to make the message even more telling: this isn't just a man saying men are comrades, as Tom Costello did, but Mum, or Sis, dressed up as a man, reinforcing the point by allowing that it is a masculine reality. The chorus of *Playmates*:

Playmates were we! Little we thought it then . . .
How we should change, when we should all be men!
Ah! sweet boyhood's days, free from all care and pain!
Playmates! Playmates! I wish we were boys again.

Of course, this is rather dreadful ('boys again', indeed, and 'free from all care and pain'), but Bessie Bonehill struck a chord: men do feel like that, and there's a measure of reality in their feeling.

What about the masculine quarrel?—the situation Wilkie

Bard epitomized in *'E ain't the bloke I took 'im for at all!*
Millie Lindon's *For old time's sake*, words and music by Charles
Osborne, points the moral here. The two men have been fight-
ing over a girl, so that 'Passion, alas, their hearts had fired':

> For old times' sake, don't let our enmity live,
> For old times' sake, say you'll forget and forgive;
> Life's too short to quarrel,
> Hearts too precious to break—
> Shake hands and let us be friends, for old times' sake.

In both the preceding numbers, the tune must really be heard
to lift the sentiment out of absurdity.

What about the quarrel between girl and boy? The girl's
message is explicit in Kate Carney's *Are we to part like this?*,
by Harry Castling and Chas Collins.

> Are we to part like this, Bill?
> Are we to part this way—
> Who's it to be,
> 'Er or me . . .
> Don't be afraid to say.
> If ev'rything's over between us, don't never pass me by;
> For you and me still friends can be, for the sake of the days
>   gone by.

Vesta Victoria, of all people, reinforces this message. One
gets so used to thinking of Vesta in ludicrous, not to say improper, numbers (*I want to play with my little Dick*, and so
forth), that it comes as a surprise—oh, what a surprise!, as
Charles Coburn would say—to find she can take a straight
number in her stride. Here's her *All in a Day*, music and words
by Joseph Tabrar.

> All in a day my 'eart grew sad,
> Misfortune came my way.
> I 'ad to learn the whole bitter truth
> All in a single day!

126

FRIENDSHIP

The bloke what I worshipp'd as I lov'd my life,
After a-saying 'e'd make me his wife,
Courtin' another young girl on the sly:
When I goes straight up to 'im, 'Look 'ere, Bill,' says I,

'Bid me good-bye forever,
Never come back no more.
Think of the 'eart you've gone and broke
Of the donah yer used to adore;
Marry the girl you fancy,
I wish you luck, I do . . .
But I mean to tarry, cos I'll never marry
If I can't be tied up to you.'

One may also mention here the friendship of the pre-adolescent boy and girl which soon, they both hope (or who-ever's singing the song does), will turn into love. Lil Haw-thorne's *I'll be your sweetheart* contains a vow of this kind, for the boy promises to be the young girl's Valentine, and ends the chorus, 'When I'm a man, my plan Will be to marry you.' (It's a bit confusing, here as quite often, that singers of either sex were apt to sing numbers as if they were of the other . . . and not only, I mean, when they were dressed up in the other's clothes. There would seem to be a marked element of bisexuality in the Music Hall art or, at any rate, the appearance of it.) Of course, when the young girl does grow up, she doesn't always feel the same way about the boy, and has to appeal to Mum for protection, as in Hylda Glyder's *Ma, he's making eyes at me!*, though perhaps—in fact probably—the girl is only being coy, and is using Ma as a decoy duck.

Before we confront the friendship of Mum and Dad when, the long matrimonial battle over, they sit holding hands beside the fire or in the workhouse, let us consider the friendship for an inanimate object—as extolled by G H Chirgwin, 1855–1922, 'The White-eyed Kaffir', no less. I have rather desperately tucked in Chirgwin at this point, because I couldn't think where else to put him—or, to be frank, didn't really

127

want to put him anywhere. He probably belongs to the earlier section on the Nigger Minstrels, for Harry Hunter, the Mohawks' Interlocutor, wrote Chirgwin's master-song, *My Fiddle is my Sweetheart,* and the illustrious 'Pony' Moore contributed his equally admired *Blind Boy.*

I have listened hopefully to Chirgwin recordings, spoken to fans who heard him, and respectfully read Willson Disher telling us that 'only Marie Lloyd was better loved by the public than he'. This, to me, is a complete mystery, for every-thing about his act seems revolting. I don't think I feel this because he 'blacked up'—dozens of artists did this, among them greats like Gene Stratton who seem entirely acceptable. Nor is it his gimmick of the diamond-shaped 'white eye' on his black make-up ... which seems as good a one as many Music Hall artists used. Nor is it his calling himself a 'kaffir' (or, earlier on, 'The White-eyed Musical Moke'), because if you object to 'kaffir', you've got to object to 'Nigger Minstrel' and a lot of other Music Hall nonsense too. No, it's just that what I have gleaned about his act makes it seem to me so dreadful, and if it was, and if it be true he was admired as much as Marie Lloyd, then I have to admit Music Hall audiences, whose taste was usually so sound, were fallible (or else that my own is, which is unthinkable).

A long and appalling verse, and then this chorus:

> My fiddle is my sweetheart,
> And I'm her faithful beau;
> I take her to my bosom
> Because I love her so.

Then comes—horror upon horror—a *yodel.* Between verses, he says 'Ladies and Gen'plum'. He actually played on a one-string fiddle, as well as the cello, violin and banjo. The voice, to use Disher's laudatory words, was 'thin and piping'—also in a falsetto half the time, as the recordings reveal. As for his *Blind Boy,* the legend went round that this was a song about his son, which it was not.

Unless I'm doing Chirgwin a great injustice, I am consoled

by reflecting that, for all of us, there is probably at least one immensely admired contemporary artist who means absolutely nothing to us. Thus, while I think popular taste is extremely accurate about pop performers, and that even when one doesn't oneself like an artist one can quite well see what his appeal is, there are also one or two whose success seems a total mystery. This may be due to a blind spot, or to a lapse in general judgement. So all I can say about Chirgwin, before going on to the more congenial topic of matrimonial friendship, is that I hope someone will write in to me and, after a due rebuke, explain what I have missed in the appalling art of the 'White-eyed Kaffir'.

Songs in praise of the golden fetters of the marriage vow are legion, from the distant days of Charles Godfrey's *The Golden Wedding* up till songs by artists who were alive only yesterday. Marie Kendall celebrated this blissful state in *Just like the ivy I'll cling to you* (Harry Castling and A J Mills), and this number, already popular in itself, acquired a heightened significance when Marie was arrested, outside the London Pavilion, for picketing during the Music Hall strike of 1907. She refused to 'move on', and was escorted to the station up the Tottenham Court road between two massive coppers, singing this number at the top of her voice and folowed by an enthusiastic crowd. Gus Elen, despite his cynicism, rallies round as well in *Me and 'Er*. I quote two verses of this, as well as their choruses (which have a significant variation when repeated), because I think they faithfully reveal the old Cockney's thoughts about marriage

We treads this parf o' life as every married couple ought,
Me and 'er—'er and me;
In fact we're looked on as the 'appiest couple down the court,
Me and 'er—'er and me.
I must acknowledge that she 'as a black eye now and then,
But she don't care a little bit, not she;
It's a token of affection—yuss, in fact that is love
Wiv me and 'er—'er and me.

For she's a lady—yuss, and I'm a gentleman,
We're boaf looked up to, and deserves ter be;
For she's a lady—yuss, and I'm a toff—
Me and 'er—'er and me.

'Cos we keeps straight, we 'as to put up wiv some sneers and
    slurs,
Me and 'er—'er and me;
Our 'oneymoon ain't over yet, though we've been married
    years,
Me and 'er—'er and me.
We don't purfess to be no better than the rest o' folks,
But the wife's a bit pertickler, don't yer see,
So we goes to church on Sunday, like the village blacksmith
    did,
Me and 'er—'er and me.

For she's a lady—yuss, and I'm a gentleman,
We're boaf looked up to, and deserves to be;
For she's a lady—yuss, and I'm 'er bloke—
Me and 'er—'er and me.

One of the many beauties of the Cockney language is that
you can rhyme 'slurs' with 'years'.

I cannot, at this point, avoid *My Old Dutch* (words and
music by Albert Chevalier himself), since this is, I suppose,
the classic ditty about conjugal fidelity. As a matter of fact,
the lyric is quite an astute one, though the tune is lugubrious,
and Chevalier delivered it with such oleaginous dollops of
sentiment that an admirer of the art of the Halls, masking
his blushes, feels he ought really to keep quiet about it. To
sing this number, Chevalier set his scene with skill. This is
what happened. To a soft whine of violins under-playing the
central theme, the tabs part and you see a drop inscribed
WORKHOUSE. In this there are cut two doors, one marked
MEN, the other WOMEN. Sitting before the drop is the workhouse porter (appearing at thirty shillings a week, since his isn't

a speaking part) when lo and behold, in totter Albert and his Dutch (she probably at twenty shillings a week, since she doesn't speak either), and Albert presents his admittance cards to the porter. This functionary glances severely at the old pair (a tremolo from the French horn now joining the violins), and indicates with a rough gesture that they must now enter the workhouse doors. But, Albert has not noticed that there are *two* entrances: and tries to go in with his ancient donah to the one marked MEN. Whereupon the porter tries to separate them roughly, and push the aged Dutch into the door marked WOMEN. The full horror of the situation dawns on Albert, who cries, 'You can't do this to *us*—we've been together FOR FORTY YEARS.' A curtain now cuts off the porter and the donah (who nip round to the pub for a half quartern), and Albert advances to the footlights, despair yet determination on his honest features and, as the orchestra moves into its big moment, thus begins:

I got a pal: a real old out-and-outer.
She's a dear good old gal, and I'll tell you all about 'er.
'Tis many years since fust we met—
'Er 'air was then as black as jet.
'Tis whiter now, but she don't fret,
Don't my old girl . . .

We've been together now for forty years,
And it don't seem a day too much—
An' there ain't a lady living in the land as I'd swap for my
    dear old Dutch!
No! There ain't . . .

and repeats the last line with intense emotion amid a roll of drums, *fortissimo* on every instrument, and hysterical sobs rising from the transported audience.

But what happens if the Old Dutch passes on (or over or out, as Mr Noël Coward has put it), leaving the old man a widower, or vice versa? Memories are still fragrant, Marie

Lloyd assures us. Here is her account in *I can't forget the days
when I was young*, music by Sam Mayo, lyric by Worton David.

> I've had my share of married life,
> Lor' lummy, not 'arf, what-oh!
> But my poor Bill went up aloft
> A couple of years ago.
> And when I scrub the bedroom out,
> And gaze beneath the bed
> At the lavender trousers that he wore
> The morning we got wed . . .
>
> Oh, I can't forget the days when I was young,
> And it don't seem so very long ago;
> When I sit for hours and stare
> At those trousers on the chair—
> Oh, I can't forget the days when I was young.

Connubial bliss amid the family and friends is also lauded:
what George Orwell, commenting on the proliferation of the
Dickensian family after marriage, compared to a swarming
oyster bed. The Great Macdermott, no less, had a number
of this nature by Ernest J Symons and N G Towers. *Sweethearts and wives* is what was called a 'kiss' number—that is,
at the point marked by 'x's' in the lyric, the singer kisses the
air (with a telling gesture of his hand towards the audience)
—which is quite hard to do, at any rate to make it audible
above the music and even sound like a kiss; so that ingenious
electricians, on radio programmes or gramophone recordings,
have found that to abruptly release a tablespoon from a
plate of blanc-mange sounds more like the real thing than
the unaided human lips.

> 'Mid the smiles of bright-eyed lasses,
> And the sight of dear old friends,
> When the merry clink of glasses
> In some jolly chorus blends,

FRIENDSHIP

At a cheerful little party
With a kind and genial host,
Oft with voices strong and hearty
Have we joined in this old Toast:

Sweethearts and Wives, Sweethearts and Wives!
Girls are the joy of all our lives.
When pretty lips kiss
x x x x,
Who can resist the Darlings?

I imagine a party at Messrs Cheerybles' being rather like this.
   C W Murphy and Harry Castling, composing jointly, wrote
a number for Charles R Whittle that sums up the whole theme
of Friendship in Music Hall terms. This has a rather haunting
melody, and I like to think of Music Hall audiences singing
it as they made their way back to Hoxton, Bermondsey, or
Bethnal Green. For as the theatre always ought to be, the
Music Halls were a place for catharsis, as well as fun. You
went there to let your hair down—though not too far down,
perhaps, as happened to Alice Leamar's unfortunate girl in
Her Golden Hair was hanging down her Back. Also, the Music
Hall audiences must have felt—and rightly, if they did—
that the Halls were something of the people by the people
for the people whereas today most pop entertainment, even
if the artists are Us, is projected on the audience by Them.

We all go the same way home—
All the collection in the same direction,
All go the same way home,
So there's no need to part at all.
We all go the same way home—
Let's be gay and hearty, don't break up the party,
We'll cling together like the ivy on the old garden wall.

Bioscope

As the audience left the Halls, around midnight, when the last live act was over, a white screen dropped and the bioscope flickered on. One can imagine the sharp lad up above the gallery operating this novelty, and perhaps feeling that even though they put him and his instrument at the bottom of the bill, his day would come.

So imagining the dim accelerated images of the bioscope, we may try to pick up some threads of the Music Hall story. Its early history still remains to be written: and I invite any reader who may have influence at one of the new universities to consider this theme as one that merits a grant for an enterprising young scholar, who would have to try to answer some tantalizing questions: chiefly, before the Halls began, round about the 1840s, since they couldn't have emerged from nothing, what were the origins, earlier on, of pop lyrics and music?

As the reader will have gathered, I can pretend to no scholarship in the account I have given—I mean to no systematic research. I have simply followed an interest and inclination over the years, and looked up what facts seemed relevant. I know I have left out a lot—there are dozens of artists, for instance, whose faces are still to be seen staring buoyantly from Music Hall song covers, and hundreds of songs mouldering in the libraries, that I haven't studied at all, though I believe I've mentioned most of the key names. But the pop song of eighty years is a vast subject, and that is why I hope some devoted young pedagogue will one day go into the whole matter thoroughly; though I do think, if he's to get anywhere worth while, he must have some feeling for the subject initially. When in the 'nineties a learned judge, hearing her name mentioned in a case before him, said, 'Who

134

is Connie Gilchrist?', what he really meant was, 'Although I'm trying this case, I don't give a damn who she is'—despite her being a renowned skipping-rope dancer of the Halls, a magician in panto in *The Forty Thieves*, and later Countess of Orkney—facts well known to everybody except for the scholar on the bench.

So how, in brief, did it all begin? Before the Halls erupted, there were certainly ballads marketed round the Seven Dials, and sung in the streets by singers trying to sell them—as I have seen, in Paris as late as the 1930s, street singers doing in Montmartre (see René Clair's early films as proof that this happened). An early example of these is *Nix my dolly pals fake away*, a criminal song about Jack Sheppard, adapted from a stage play of 1839. (The word 'dolly', by the way, is still used by older East End characters as a synonym for 'mate'.) We also know—and here, yet again, I am cribbing from Willson Disher—that there were 'catch' and 'glee' clubs as early as the 'forties, and in the 'fifties 'song clubs' such as the Coal Hole, Fountain Court, Strand, or Cribbs' in Panton street, Haymarket. Sessions of popular song also took place at the Cyder Cellars, Maiden lane, at Sadler's Wells, the Rotunda, Vauxhall gardens, and various Harmonic Halls and Assembly Rooms.

Among primitives of the Music Halls we have already heard of W G Ross who sang *Sam Hall* at the Cyder Cellars, of Frederick Robson who sang *Villikins and his Dinah* at the Grecian Saloon, of Sam Cowell, also of the Grecian and the Cremorne, who sang *The Ratcatcher's Daughter*, and of Sam Collins who offered Irish numbers at Evans's Song and Supper Rooms in Covent Garden. Some of these places, like Evans's, were patronized by the respectable, others, like the Cyder Cellars, less so. These singers were in their prime in the 1850s, and had already departed by the 'sixties.

At the same time, we have noticed that Charles Morton had built the Canterbury in 1849, so that the 'fifties would seem to be the decade of transition from singing clubs, of a sociable rather than a theatrical nature, to music halls, which were associated with a tavern, presided over by the Chairman, and which aimed at a greater public and commercial appeal. The Chairman soon became a key figure—often, in fact, the principal artist—as Harry Fox, or 'Red Nose', when he presided over the Old Mo.

Concurrently, the Nigger Minstrels were also getting into their stride, introducing American performers and a trans-atlantic idiom, and while also singing initially in the clubs like the local singers, preparing to take over their own non-alcoholic halls. Thus E W Mackney (1825–1909), 'The Cele-brated Negro Delineator', sang at Evans's with Sam Cowell, as well as with Minstrel troupes. The Minstrel routine became established, with the singers sitting in a row facing the audience, blacked up and wearing striped trousers, and with some ten musicians brandishing bones, banjos and tam-bourines. The figure corresponding to the new Music Hall Chairman was the Interlocutor, who quizzed the Corner Men, or Endmen, with heavy-handed question-and-answer jests (the answer repeating the question, and the next question, the answer), delivered in what passed for southern Negro speech. Since the jokes were laborious, and the songs lugubrious, the whole effect was 'improving', as titles of troupes like *The McNish, Johnson and Slaven's Refined Minstrels* may suggest.

As the Halls swung into their stride, women began to appear, though it wasn't till the 'seventies that stars emerged, of which the most notable was Jenny Hill (1850–96), known as 'The Vital Spark', who was a cabby's daughter married to an acrobat. Her most notable number as a *serio comic* is *The Coffee-shop Girl*, though she also indulged in male im-personations, thus setting a style so often to be imitated later on. An even more popular favourite was Bessie Bellwood (1857–96), born Bessie Mahoney, beloved of uncouth audiences, with whom she would take part in slanging matches from stage to gods. Her most applauded number was *Wot Cheer, Riah!* (this is really the Cockney 'wotcher'), but though one cannot doubt the power of the legend of its immense effectiveness, the song seems, in cold print, fairly feeble.

It is pleasant to think of the girls getting a chance at last, because until the Halls threw open their welcoming doors, the outlets in the legitimate theatre must have been limited (especially for uneducated women) and, apart from marriage, there wasn't much to choose from except being a servant, working in a factory, signing on with Florence Nightingale or becoming a nun (or of course a harlot). Plaques are placed on houses where the first women doctors (or whatever) lived, as symbols of the emancipation of their sex, but perhaps one should go up to Bessie Bellwood; for by the end of the century, women Music Hall artists—and of course Gaiety girls and ballet dancers in the Strand and Leicester Square—were making a lot of money and having a fine old time; and also, of course, giving immense pleasure to millions. Mrs Siddons has a rather dreary statue in Paddington Green (now dwarfed additionally by the new flyover) about whose *Pretty Polly Perkins* Harry Clifton used to sing. I can't think off-hand of any other monument to an actress in London, though Marie Lloyd has her pub; so if anyone feels like contributing to a carving of Bessie Bellwood (or even Bessie Bonehill in uniform waving *The Old Tattered Flag*), we could try and get up a committee.

By now we have entered the period—from the 'seventies onwards—that I have covered more fully in the earlier sections, but there still remain one or two notable artists who have somehow got left out—chiefly, I must admit, because despite their fame, I haven't been able to find out much about them. Thus, Annie Adams, a mountainous *serio comic*, was apparently much admired for a number which began 'He played on the Indian drum-drum-drum', and ended 'And made a terrible noise'—which one can well believe. James Henry Stead, who wore a striped suit, a conical cap, and a goatee beard, was notable for bouncing up and down rigidly hundreds of times to the chorus of his songs:

137

this was known—for reasons I have not been able to fathom
—as 'The Cure'. Jolly John Nash, who dressed as a 'chappie'
like Leybourne, was noted for a number which began

Hi Hi! Here stop!
Waiter, waiter, fizzy pop!

which was apparently much admired by the Prince of Wales.
Cinquavelli was the great juggler (this art is still to be seen
in some Palladium shows—it must be one of the longest-
surviving in show-biz history), and the Griffiths Brothers were
the two classic halves of the panto horse.

Let us consider now the people who, apart from the singers
(and their impresarios), contributed so much to the success
of the Halls. Readers will surely have noticed, in the names
of composer and lyric writer I have put after most of the
famous songs, how frequently the same names crop up
again and again. This is indeed the case: it is astonishing how
many winners some of these bards wrote, and in what a
variety of styles. Their fecundity is also remarkable, though
they probably had to write a lot, for until the copyright laws
were introduced payment for a song was cash down—Fred
Gilbert, for instance, got £10 without royalties from Coburn
for *The Man who broke the Bank at Monte Carlo*. It would seem
many of these men did other jobs as well—they would need
to at those rates of pay—being perhaps journalists if lyric
writers, and musical performers if composers. One is also
struck by their higher level of education than that of most of
the artists. This is of course frequently the case—for instance
Laurence Hart, apart from being a descendant of Heine,
was, in the numbers he wrote for Richard Rodgers and their
singers, a considerable minor poet in his own right. I think
it is also worth noting that there appear to have been no
women lyricists or composers, despite there being as many
female singers as men. I can't think of any convincing reason
for this—and can only add the supposition that women
singers probably did, in reality, have a lot to do with the

138

writing of the songs, since I imagine they often worked on
the draft of a number somebody had sold to them. As to
the literary influences on the Music Hall lyrics—if one can
speak of such—I would suspect W S Gilbert among others,
and possibly Kipling in Edwardian days ... though it may
be he was as much influenced by the Halls as they might
have been by him: for it is known he visited Gatti's-under-
the-Arches when he lived in Villiers street, and one of his
poems is about a Music Hall star. But I think the chief
'influence' on the lyric writers is that of popular speech itself.
For the best of them had an extremely deft ear, so that their
numbers never seem forced or condescending but entirely
natural and convincing.

As for the composers, I have not sufficient knowledge of
music to be able to suggest where they got their musical ideas
from—this could be another theme for investigation by my
imaginary young researcher. In some of the earliest works,
like *Villikins and his Dinah* and *The Boy in the Gallery*, there
is a distant echo of English folk music, as there is also sometimes, despite their later date, in Lauder's Scottish numbers.
I suspect German pop music was a strong influence—it is
noticeable how frequently the best tunes are waltz numbers,
and I imagine the composers listened to Viennese operetta.
Another influence I strongly suspect is that of Salvation Army
tunes, and of Protestant hymns in general. This may seem at
first a strange suggestion, but I think in fact Music Hall and
the Salvation Army had much in common. They were both
spontaneous pop working class creations, largely outside the
area of middle and upper class culture, and they both relied
heavily on songs to put over their message. For example: if
you know the tune of Albert Chevalier's *My Old Dutch*, try
leaving out the words, and putting in 'sacred' ones of your
own invention ... and hey presto! it's at once a hymn (and
a better hymn, I think, than a Music Hall number). I believe
the fact is that Cavaliers and Roundheads, and Merrie Eng-
landers and Puritans, are far closer together than they may
imagine, since both are enthusiastic about something; and

that in this case, the Music Hall is a sort of lay version of popular evangelism.[1]

When we consider the production of individual lyric writers and composers, we shall see how gifted some of these were. If the reader will take my word for it that all the songs I have quoted are Music Hall 'standards', then to give an idea of how prolific and versatile some of these artists were, I have counted up the number of times a writer or composer mentioned in the text has collaborated in at least three famous songs sung by at least three different artists. This test, of course, is a bit hard on those who wrote chiefly for one singer, or whose numbers, though excellent, I haven't quoted at all. (It also excludes singers who composed for themselves, like Lauder and Chevalier.) We get the following result:

Lyric writer or composer	Songs	Artists
George Arthurs	3	3
Edgar Bateman	3	3
Harry Castling	6	4
Chas Collins	6	5
Worton David	4	4
Fred Gilbert	4	4
George Le Brunn	6	4
Fred W Leigh	11	8
C W Murphy	7	4
A J Mills	3	3
Felix McGlennon	4	3
Bennett Scott	3	3
Leslie Stuart	3	3

What strikes me, in fact, about the composers of the songs is that just as there are fewer dramatists than actors, so there are far fewer great lyric writers and musicians than there are singers.

Nor should we forget the artists of the sheet music covers.

[1] The English must be the only people in the world who would find nothing incongruous in singing *Rock of Ages* before a championship football match.

These are not only often beautiful in themselves, but their
vivacity and attention to detail help to form a picture of the
performers, and of the kind of song they were presenting; for
the singer is usually drawn 'in character' on the cover. English
graphic art was unusually rich in the 19th century, and the
work of the draughtsmen hovers agreeably between pop and
'fine' art ... Keene, for instance, much admired by Degas,
was a draughtsman who appealed to both worlds—in periodi-
cals as well as exhibitions—though I do not think he worked
for the song publishers at all. But Cruickshank and Dicky
Doyle, among others, did. Their song covers are in black and
white, and the most notable artist in colour is Alfred Concannen, who drew dozens of covers from the 'sixties to the
'eighties, for songs by forgotten artists as well as for those
of lasting fame like Leybourne, Vance, Johnny Danvers,
Charles Godfrey and Harry Clifton. Concannen's modest and
effective art has long been rescued from oblivion, and there
are avid collectors of his song sheets which are as arresting
for their portrait of a society as for their apt and exquisite
style. John Braudard drew in an earlier period, from the
'fifties to the 'sixties, in a more romantic vein. Later on, in
the 'seventies, came H G Banks, more down to earth than
Concannen, and designer of covers for many of the singers
mentioned in this study. After the decline of the Halls, there
was a period of total banality in song covers, but today,
when L P sleeves have replaced them as the principal means
of projecting the songs visually, a new pop art of great variety
and beauty has arisen.

Then there were the theatres. With the final disappearance
of the Metropolitan, Edgware road, two years ago, it is now
no longer possible to see what a London Hall looked like,
though some Halls built before 1900 still survive in the provinces. To try to give an idea of what the bigger Halls were
like, let us consider the Alhambra, which stood till the 1930s
on the present site of the Odeon, Leicester square. It began
in 1854, already in a 'Moorish' style, as the Royal Panopticon
offering performances intended 'to assist by moral and

intellectual agencies the best interests of society'. It then
became a wax works. Next, one E J Smith, an impresario,
re-built it with—wonder of wonders—an 'ascending carriage',
or lift, and internal fountains. It then became a circus. Next
a Music Hall and restaurant over whose tables Leotard, *The
Daring Young Man on the Flying Trapeze*, swung for £180 a
week without a net between himself and the diners. Then it
put on ballet, with an orchestra of sixty and four hundred
performers, but when it introduced the can-can in the 'sixties,
had its licence removed by the Middlesex magistrates. Next
came opera and promenade concerts, a fire, a rebuilding in
1883 as the Alhambra Theatre Royal, and a change the
following year to the Alhambra Theatre of Varieties. In 1884,
too, the Empire opened on the north side of the square, and
in 1887 also became a Music Hall. Here Yvette Guilbert
played in 1894, followed by Cissie Loftus, La Belle Otéro, and
ballet with Genée as star for ten years after 1897. The Empire
was famous for its Promenade, from which you could see
the show and, from closer to, courtesans who spent the
evening there waiting for you to offer them a b. and s. or
some bubbly. This delightful and harmless place came to be
thought by moralists so scandalous that a trellis was erected
between the Promenade and the theatre proper, which was
soon torn down indignantly by young bloods, among them
Winston Churchill. Thanks to the indefatigable machinations
of one Mrs Ormiston Chant, who launched a virulent cam-
paign against it, the Promenade was eliminated around World
War I.

I do not think it can be denied that the Alhambra and the
Empire theatres were more attractive places than the Odeon
and Empire cinemas now (or as the Empire in its most recent
manifestation as a decorous dance hall). Of course, the
showing of films doesn't need a lavish décor, for the illusion
proceeds entirely from the screen, and not at all from wherever
the movie happens to be shown; and a cinema public is essentially a mass of units, each imbibing his personal message,
and not an audience. (One can quite happily see a film in a

cinema alone, but unless one were Ludwig of Bavaria, a theatrical performance for an audience of one would not be very enjoyable on either side of the footlights.) It is also true that a film offers far greater variety, or dimensions, of dream, since its images can travel anywhere in the world ... the theatre, by comparison, however splendid, is sweaty, provincial and rather silly. But it is more human in an immediate sense and, for this reason, its impact at moments can be profounder.

Though a handful of live theatres survive, modern variety comes to us mostly through films, television, radio and recordings. Perhaps that means that we can now see more of it, even if at secondhand, than our great-grandfathers who relied on the local Hall. Though even this I am inclined to doubt, at any rate so far as artists appearing in England go. For it is remarkable how the Music Hall performers got around, and if you went, say, to the Cosmotheka every Saturday night, you probably saw all the best of them within a number of years. So that I think the gain in wider projection today is offset by the loss of personal contact. For I don't think anyone could maintain that seeing Frankie Howerd on the telly is as intimate an experience as seeing Little Tich in an actual Hall.

If my rather arbitrary date of 1920 for the end of the Halls is accepted, there did survive into the ensuing decades (apart, that is, from the 'veterans of variety' kind of revival I mentioned earlier) a number of artists who though they belonged to a younger generation than the authentic stars, embodied something of their spirit: Max Miller, Bud Flanagan, Gracie Fields, Randolph Sutton, Sid Field, Lupino Lane, Ernie Lotinga, Dickie Henderson, George Formby Junior, the Houston Sisters and Whimsical Walker among others. All these artists, though they appeared in other media, were at their best in front of a live audience and seemed to need the feeling of direct communication with their public which was essential to the spirit of the Halls—which still survived, up till World War II, in such places as the Holborn Empire, the Victoria Palace, the Palladium,[1] and, in the provinces, the Argyll, Birkenhead. And all these artists, because they could deal with both the older world of pop art and the new, were able to transmit to later performers such elements of Music Hall as could be adapted to changing times, and so in part influence and continue them. For just as the Music Halls were not born overnight in the 1840s, so did they linger, though disappearing, into the 1920s and beyond.

There is, of course, always the fallacy of supposing the old art was better because it is dead, and one must be constantly on guard against this. It is true that any art of the past has a legitimate period charm: however much you admire a cathedral, say, for its intrinsic architectural quality, you can scarcely ignore the reality that it may also appeal to you because it has a period flavour. Yet in comparing an older art with one of the present, one should not attach undue value to this. For what matters most, I think, in judging the quality of an art of any past period, is to try to assess it as it was in its own day, and then compare its achievement with that of the equivalent art of your own.

Both Music Hall and modern variety, being pop arts, were concerned basically with the same thing: with entertaining their society, making money out of it and, to some extent, revealing it, by satire and emotion, to itself. Because the periods were so different, the means were, and we might try to weigh up what these differences are. Some of them I have hinted at already, so that what ensues is by way of a recap.

The comedians aren't singers as they used to be, or not usually so. Of if they are singers, they are not also comedians —using this word in the larger sense of someone who by his art comments upon life.

---

[1] It is curious that the Palladium, which was never an important Hall in any historic sense, should have survived all others, even till today. One might compare it to the Duchy of Leichtenstein, a once insignificant principality of the Holy Roman Empire, which has nevertheless hung on when all others have vanished.

Women play a less important part than they used to. Female comedians are now quite rare, and even among pop singers, they are in a marked minority. In the days of the Halls, it was about 50–50, though with a slight preponderance of men. (This seems rather a curious commentary on any notion that fifty years ago, or more, women were more repressed.)

Almost without exception, the Music Hall artists were from the working class. Today, most pop artists still are, but less exclusively so, and their tone tends more and more towards the petty bourgeois. This is possibly due to the general decline in the homogeneity of the working class in England.[1]

There is a cult of youth among pop artists today which did not exist in the Halls. All Music Hall artists started young, as I have said; but though many declined, or were forgotten as they grew older, this by no means always happened, and it was not in any way thought indispensable to be young. Since the youth cult is only about ten years old, it is of course hard to predict if young artists will be rejected later on simply because they are so no longer. I am inclined to doubt this, and remember foretelling, ten years ago, that Tommy Steele, for instance, because of his rare talent, would be a star at any age. He is now nearly thirty, and still is.

Modern pop is more cosmopolitan than the art of the Halls. I hope I have made quite clear that the American influence on English Music Hall dates from the 1850s, and never ceased to be considerable. Yet the artists of the Halls

---

[1] Or possibly to the emergence, in the past two decades, of an entirely new class in England. Although no one likes these terms, I think the categories of upper, middle, lower-middle and working are still valid. But there seems to be appearing yet another category, which one might describe as 'upper-working'. Many young pop performers, and their fans, seem to belong to this. Education, money, travel, social mobility, plus the loss of respect for, or even interest in, the traditional 'upper orders' may account for this. Thus, when one sees them with their working-class parents, they no longer seem to 'belong'; though I'm not of course suggesting any snobbery, or rejection, in their attitudes to Mum and Dad. It's just that their interests have become so different and even—quite apart from dress—their looks.

remained, I think, more indelibly English than modern English pop artists do. This does not, I would say, apply to the modern artists' personalities, but to their performance. No one would take the Beatles and the Stones for anything but English (or Irish) boys, but their singing style is Anglo-American. If Lauder, or Chevalier, or Marie Lloyd went to America, as they all did, it was to show something English, and sell it as such. If a modern pop group goes to the U S, it is to show something 'anglo-saxon' in the sense that President de Gaulle uses this term.

Thus, English pop art today is less English than French pop art is French. I believe this is simply due to a matter of language, plus modern means of reproduction. Since the French have their own tongue, they tend to develop, despite alien influences, a much more particular style. But English minstrels, to whom L Ps of American performers are not only immediately available, but easily comprehensible, tend to be influenced by them more. In addition, French poets—if only minor ones—have always been interested in pop art, whereas our own have only recently become so, and rather self-consciously at that. Conversely, French pop artists have often sung songs by their own poets, or even, like Trenet, been minor poets themselves. This means that French singers have an additional source of purely French inspiration; whereas our own, though they write excellent numbers (which in turn sometimes influence the Americans), do so in a more hybrid, international style. A pop artist like Yvette Guilbert who had a repertoire of thousands of songs by poets classical and modern, would be inconceivable in England. This is possibly the 'fault' (if one can speak of 'faults') of English audiences, who like wit and sentiment, but not passion or ideas.

Modern pops are far more impersonal than the older ones. I think stunning English songs are written today, and their delivery is often riveting, but that few would stand up alone in print. Idea and emotion, such as they are, have become generalized. One can remember the titles of many modern songs, and what they sounded like, but rarely what or who they were about.

A direct contact between artist and audience has gone. I am far from praising the past at the cost of the present, and infinitely prefer the future to either; but objectively, I think one must allow that to see modern pop groups on telly, or even with tens of thousands in the Shea stadium, is not so personal an experience as hearing artists in a Hall holding only some hundreds. Nor does the human voice, mechanically reproduced, sound at all the same as when it is heard directly. Mme Callas may be marvellous on an L P, and indeed is, but the sound one hears at Covent Garden is utterly different. This is not at all to deny that mikes and studio recording gear can be used by a skilful artist to create new effects which the unaided human voice cannot. But I don't think these effects are so lastingly compelling. 'I love you' sounds miraculous over the phone, but even better face to face in a room.

It would of course be nice if we could get the best of both worlds—hear pop artists of our own day in intimate surroundings. In the last decade, there was a revival of pop singing in pubs, much of it of a very high standard. This looked for a moment like a return to the Grecian Saloon before anyone thought of building the Royal Eagle. But hardly had the new talents emerged, when telly descended on the scene, and to the embryo of personal involvement was administered the instant contraceptive pill of mass entertainment. And this, I am inclined to think, is what most of us really want now. We may be seduced by the idea of hearing the original blues singer sitting on the levee with his bare feet dangling into the Old Mo, but we'd really rather listen to him boxed up or sleeved into an L P. (As for the blues singer, he'd probably prefer that too.)

In yet another sense, we also participate less. In the days of the Halls, if you wanted to get to know the song, you had to buy the sheet music and sit down at a piano and learn it (or else go to hear Coburn flogging his number so metronomically that you could learn it that way). Learning a song from a recording or a juke-box isn't quite the same process: it goes straight into your ear, but doesn't come through your body. In other words, I think our great-grandfathers were more performers of music than we . . . though among younger generations, thanks to the proliferation of guitars, this may no longer be the case.

Lastly, I think that modern pops are concerned with only one possible function of a song. A pop song, in a mild way, can both reveal and teach. It creates for you a kind of epitome of what you had vaguely felt hitherto, and impresses you by making these feelings clearer and more explicit. Then it can also tell you—or suggest to you—by both tune and lyrics, what you could feel about what it has revealed—a message, of course, that you can take or leave as you please. Modern pops certainly encourage you to feel, but not much to think about why you feel what you do. Music Hall songs, at their best, offer both emotion and reflection. Many may consider that the absence of a 'moral' in modern pops is an advantage: but I think it does remove one possible dimension of a number. A blues song, for example, will make the singer's comment about what he feels as clear as the emotion that arouses it.[1]

The decline of the Halls was not only due to technical factors, though these were important: film, radio, gramophone mike, telly came too late to do much damage to what was already dying. Nor, I think, to stylistic changes: ragtime and jazz, revue and musical comedy. Nor yet to economic forces: palaces of variety, twice-nightly shows, more money for the stars, less for the meteors. Nor altogether to the Music Hall's own efforts to destroy itself—as all dying arts are inclined

---

[1] Re-reading this, I don't think it's now correct. When pop songs first hit England, in the mid 'fifties, most of them *were* rather meaningless, so far as lyric went; and if you wanted a 'message', you had to listen to now-vanished skiffle, or the portentous and rather priggish social commentaries of the 'folk' singers. But within the past year or so, sub-groups in the pop world – especially in the States – have increasingly used this musical medium to put over 'messages' of various social sorts. Even the Beatles developed, in their later songs, from the 'Yeah, yeah' verbal banality of their earlier numbers to songs in which ideas were projected.

to do—from within: Karno introducing mimed 'gang' shows in place of the individual character act, increasingly spectacular displays at Halls like the Hippodrome, or the dead weight of Harry Lauder uplift. Nor is the decline due to the intervention of Mrs Ormiston Chant, and censors who disapproved of 'music hall jokes' that they had really heard from saloon bar wags.

I believe the real cause of the decline was chiefly social. Up till World War I, England had, despite considerable changes, a more or less stratified social structure. From the time of the Lloyd George reforms onwards, the classes became fragmented to a far greater extent, and this process was violently accentuated by World War I. Class distinctions did survive, as they still do: but they could no longer be seen in terms of absolutes. Now, the Music Hall was an art not of social protest—that would be claiming far too much for it— but it was an art of working-class social self-assertion. At the same time—and rather contradictorily—it was, despite its ironies about the class structure, basically acceptive of this established social order. So that when this structure cracked, both because of political reform, wartime social mobility, and an increasing scepticism about the nation's rulers, both the driving force of self-assertion, and the conventions of a traditional class structure, lost much of their force. To these we must add that the loss of 1 million service men, the revolt in Ireland, the mounting troubles in the decaying empire, and the financial instability following the war, deprived the singers and their audiences of much of that faith in themselves and their country which they held, however blindly and unrealistically, up till the great war. A blues or a flamenco singer thrives on disaster—as an artist, that is, if not as a human being. But the Music Hall artists could not, because the absence of passion and deeper social realism in the Music Hall tradition deprived them of any means to express anger, and left them emotionally high and dry.

So anyone who feels that the English working class were

happier and better off materially in the years after World War I, need not shed a single tear for the disappearance of the Halls. This is, in the end, my own feeling about their art, despite a real admiration and fondness for its qualities. I cannot regret a society in which Harry Champion dreamed of boiled beef and carrots while Colonel North held his princely garden party, where Kate Carney's boy bought her a penn'orth of each while the Johnnies had all the Cliquot, Cliquot, or where Gus Elen's back yard had turnip tops and cabbages while Lord Roseb'ry inherited and married two fortunes. Everything I hear of the Edwardian era convinces me it was one of the most revolting periods in our history—vulgar, bullying and obtuse—and one of the many reasons I like the Music Hall artists so much is that they managed to put up with it. At the same time, I don't think it can be denied that if you had the good fortune then to live in the upper fringe of working class society, you did have a darn good time if you could manage to forget—as you probably could —that this tenuous prosperity was based on the want of millions in England and its far-flung empire. And yet another reason why the Music Hall singers didn't want to delve too deep is probably that they were rising out of the abyss themselves, or had already risen, and didn't want to look back.

The paradox seems to be that you don't get a really great pop art except in conditions of extreme misery—that is, short of total destitution, when no one would feel like singing anyway. When Negroes are slaves, they sing spirituals; when they were half slaves, they sang jazz; when they are really free—socially, economically, politically—they'll doubtless listen instead to other entertainers, and lose many artistic qualities that come out of their anguish. And one of the reasons why pop singing today is so impersonal, is probably that if the boys playing the guitars know they're richer (far richer) than the kids getting frantic in their audience, they also know full well those boys and girls don't want for bed, board, and sharp clobber.

So by the highest standards of popular art, Music Hall

doesn't rate high, I think. Beside our own folk songs (by which I do not mean contemporary 'folk', which has a strong sniff of emotional slumming about it), or Negro blues, or Spanish flamenco, or even many Continental pops of the same period, Music Hall songs don't amount to much. They're too inhibited emotionally, too limited intellectually, too frankly commercial in their intentions. I think the highest one can claim for them is that they are a sort of bastard folk song of an industrial-commercial-imperial age, and perhaps their greatest virtue is that their qualities and limitations do tell us a lot about that age. For in this respect we are like birds, and the songs our people care for are an immediate indication of what they feel and think, or fail to.

In the radio programmes I mentioned at the beginning, we played the series in and out with George Ware's *The Boy in the Gallery*. This has an exquisite melody which, as I said earlier, has something of a folk tune, and something of an early Music Hall pop: a sort of missing link between the traditional and the commercial. Clarence Wright suggested, for the final performance, that he might whistle the chorus, as well as sing it. There was some doubt about the propriety of this, partly because whistling is hard to record without distortion, and also because we felt that, despite its popularity in Music Hall days, whistling is now deemed an ear-splitting vulgarity, as indeed it can be. We did however feel that this would be appropriate, not only because the Gallery boy used to signify approval of an artist with a whistle (as his descendant Mod or Rocker still does today), but also because whistling, in days when songs were transmitted from person to person, was a favourite way of spreading the glad new sound around. That this was so is proved by the pained complaints, recorded by Mr Punch, about 'errand boys' perpetually whistling. What they were in fact doing was conveying the latest of Marie Lloyd's, or Gus Elen's, by Cockney bush telegraph to their mates and donahs.

There are no errand boys now (unless in a pop group called The Deliverers), and the art of whistling died with Albert

SWEET SATURDAY NIGHT

Whelan; but Clarence Wright got his way, and nobody wrote
in to complain. The words that go with the tune are,

> The boy I love is up in the gallery,
> The boy I love is looking down at me—
> There he is, can't you see him?
> A-waving of his handkerchief
> As merry as a robin that sings on a tree.

Index of Names

Adams, Annie, 137
Archer, William, 51
Arthurs, George, 25, 105, 140
Austin, Charles, 96

Baden-Powell, General, 80
Ball, Harry, 78
Banks, H G, 141
Bard, Wilkie, 47, 57, 104–105, 115, 121, 126
Barnes (Songwriter), 119
Barnes, Fred, 11, 45
Bastow, George, 80
Bateman, Edgar, 36, 37, 53, 54, 55, 140
Beatles, the, 99, 146
Beauchamp, George, 44
Bedford, Harry, 29
Beerbohm, Max, 10, 25, 27, 47, 64, 68
Bellwood, Bessie, 136, 137
Bennett, Billy, 40, 97–98
Bernhardt, Sarah, 12, 17, 27
Bonehill, Bessie, 79, 125, 137
Booth, General, 22
Braudard, John, 141
Bruant, Aristide, 39
Bryan, V P, 123
Buller, General, 80
Burge, Mrs Dick, 15, 27
Burgess, Frederick, 34

Callas, Maria, 147
Campbell, Herbert, 51, 67, 68, 69, 70
Carnegie, Andrew, 86
Carney, Kate, 11, 28–30, 37, 109, 112, 126
Castling, Harry, 37, 58, 98, 126, 129, 133, 140
Champion, Harry, 11, 14, 17, 19, 41–42, 55, 91, 100, 109
Chant, Mrs Ormiston, 142, 149

Chaplin, Charles, 18, 35, 82, 88–90
Chaplin, Charles (Senior), 115
Chevalier, Albert, 30–31, 36, 84, 117, 130–131, 139, 140
Chevalier, Maurice, 30
Chirgwin, G H, 34, 46, 127–129
Christy, Edwin P, 34
Christy Minstrels, 117
Churchill, Winston, 84, 142
Cinquavelli, 138
Clair, René, 135
Clifton, Harry, 91, 137, 141
Coburn, Charles, 87, 91, 117, 126
Coffin, Hayden, 79
Collins, Charles, 25, 37, 43, 55, 57, 108, 126, 140
Collins, Sam, 40, 100, 135
Concannen, Alfred, 141
Connor, T W, 44
Costello, Tom, 14, 45, 77, 101, 125
Courtney, Percy, 24
Coward, Noël, 131
Cowell, Sam, 40, 135, 136
Coyne, Fred, 119
Crook, J, 31
Cruickshank, 141

Dacre, Harry, 119
Danvers, Billy, 11
Danvers, Johnny, 51, 66, 67, 70, 141
Darewski, Herman E (Junior), 107
David, Worton, 105, 132, 140
Davis, Fred, 45
de Freece, Maurice, 49
Dillon, Bernard, 24
Disher, M Willson, 19, 93, 128, 135
Dodd, Ken, 99
Dormer, Dainty Daisy, 100
Doyle, Dicky, 141
Dryden, Leo, 45, 77, 81, 101
Dunville, T E, 47, 113, 114
Duprez, Mary Moore, 115

153

INDEX

INDEX

155

INDEX

INDEX

Index of Songs

INDEX

INDEX

INDEX